Shingle Style Architecture for the 21st Century

E. Ashley Rooney

with foreword by George Fellner

Schiffer Publishing Ltd
4880 Lower Valley Road · Atglen, Pennsylvania 19310

Other Schiffer Books by the Author:
Shingle Style Homes: Past & Present, 978-0-7643-2554-0, $39.95
Asian Influenced Architecture, 978-0-7643-3383-5, $34.99
Barn Again, 978-0-7643-3431-3, $34.99
Cliffhangers and Hillside Homes: Views from the Treetops, 978-0-7643-2387-3, $39.95

Other Schiffer Books on Related Subjects:
Arts and Crafts Houses, 978-0-7643-3670-6, $45.00

Front Cover: Albert, Righter & Tittman, Courtesy of Greg Premru (main); Living Spaces Architectural Associates, Veodao Nu Bunnag (left); and Andreozzi Architect, Aaron Usher III (right)

Spine: Courtesy of Marcus Glaysteen

Back Cover: Courtesy of © Dan Gair/Blind Dog Photo, Inc. (top left); © 2009 Warren Patterson Photography (top right); Aaron Usher III (lower left); and Todd Caverly (lower right)

Title Page: Courtesy of Veodao Nu Bunnag (left) and Jeffrey Allen (right)

Library of Congress Control Number: 2010931603

Designed by RoS
Type set in Tiza/Myriad Pro

ISBN: 978-0-7643-3551-8
Printed in China

Published by Schiffer Publishing Ltd.
4880 Lower Valley Road
Atglen, PA 19310
Phone: (610) 593-1777; Fax: (610) 593-2002
E-mail: Info@schifferbooks.com

For the largest selection of fine reference books on this and related subjects, please visit our web site at **www.schifferbooks.com**
We are always looking for people to write books on new and related subjects. If you have an idea for a book please contact us at the above address.

This book may be purchased from the publisher.
Include $5.00 for shipping.
Please try your bookstore first.
You may write for a free catalog.

In Europe, Schiffer books are distributed by
Bushwood Books
6 Marksbury Ave.
Kew Gardens
Surrey TW9 4JF England
Phone: 44 (0) 20 8392 8585; Fax: 44 (0) 20 8392 9876
E-mail: info@bushwoodbooks.co.uk
Website: www.bushwoodbooks.co.uk

Contents

Foreword

Shingle Style Revival as Timeless Architecture

by George Fellner, AIA, principal, Fellner Associates Architects, Higganum, Connecticut

The study of an architectural style typically reveals a type that represents a quantifiable period of time. However, one particular style stands apart, disclosing an enduring approach to home design. The Shingle Style house was born in the early 1870s with an initial twenty-year surge. It shifted geographically from New England to other regions and steadily dwindled down while other styles attained popularity. Sparking off again in the second half of the twentieth century, a series of Shingle Style revivals have evolved, extending to the present time. This incredible range of a nearly 140-year lifespan suggests that there is a quintessential timelessness inherent with this style. It is important to note that Yale University architectural historian Vincent Scully is responsible for establishing a vast body of knowledge on this subject, starting with his book *The Shingle Style and the Stick Style (1955).* Subsequently, his *The Shingle Style Today* or *The Historian's Revenge* (1974), and his introduction in *The Architecture of the American Summer: The Flowering of the Shingle Style* (1989) followed his initial work.

The prelude to this book, *Shingle Style Houses: Past and Present,* by E. Ashley Rooney, with John McConnell and Turner Brooks, presents a comprehensive text and visual study of the manifestations of the Shingle Style. John McConnell's foreword in that book describes the role of the original Shingle Style within the context of this country's architectural history, as well as its influence on successive periods. E. Ashley Rooney's introduction describes the Shingle Style in the context of the human perspective, both past and present, and her depiction of over 50 case study homes illustrates the elaborate diversity of types and locations. In turn, through his sample projects, Turner Brooks presents a smorgasbord of Shingle Style descendents.

In a sense, this sequel, *Shingle Style Architecture for the 21st Century,* continues the story. In order to attempt an understanding of the rationale for the timelessness of the Shingle Style, a review of the historical perspective is both a necessary and a useful prerequisite. The roots of this style were seeded in the joint efforts of Andrew Jackson Davis and Andrew Jackson Downing in the 1840s, promoting the notion of the cottage house. Their series of published pattern books in the 1840s helped direct the public consciousness towards the idea of the quaint and picturesque home within a country setting. This awareness, in addition to the blended mix of the Queen Anne, Richardsonian Romanesque, Arts and Crafts, Late Medieval Country, Colonial, Carpenter Gothic, and the Stick Styles, led to the development of the Shingle Style.

The post-Civil War period accommodated the growth within the middle class of a wealthy segment of society. Initially, they were drawn to New England coastal towns, seeking a lifestyle with a sense of leisure and relaxation. From the early 1870s through the 1890s, these new clients hired the prominent architects of the day to design their country homes. The idea of the picturesque house blossomed in a uniquely American style encompassing expansive, informal interiors and variably shaped wall and roof forms wrapped in continuous wood shingles, often sited to celebrate magnificent views. Shingle Style homes continued to be built throughout the 1920s. Although their popularity steadily decreased as other styles gained attention, future revivals repeatedly demonstrated the Shingle Style home's enduring attractiveness.

Based on requirements for open and flexible spaces that flowed together, a new mindset for interior planning was born. The resulting organization of spaces created a multitude of possibilities for the creative assemblage of irregular, often asymmetric forms. In turn, the undulating facades were capped with intersecting cross-gable roof forms, secondary hips, sheds, multi-form dormers, eyebrows, and curved sections, often with multi-level eaves. Proudly bulging as focal points, polygonal or round turrets were integrated with the main volume. Extensive wraparound porches pushed and pulled on the exterior enclosure, offering multiple options for outside leisure and recreation. For the external envelope, the wall and roof cladding was typically composed of continuous wood shingles with occasional decorative patterns. Stone was often used for covering the lower story, foundation, turrets, porch supports, and sometimes arched entries. As a whole, the overall massing attempted to evoke the surrounding landscape, contextually relating the house with the site as well as the region. Furthermore, prominent chimneys, Palladian as well as single and grouped windows, bays, and balconies, with subtle detailing, contributed to the total package. Within the interiors, the detailing of the woodwork, reflecting Craftsman and an assortment of other architectural styles, carried through this high level of design and construction.

This experimentation with variations on a theme was practiced by Henry Hobson Richardson; William Ralph Emerson; McKim, Mead, and White; Greene and Greene; and numerous other architects of the period. Vincent Scully summarizes the essence of the Shingle Style:

> So the houses were both new and old, freely serving and suggesting every kind of domestic relaxation while at the same time linking modern life with an American past seemingly more primordial than it had ever been... It all added up to an eloquent architectural language, free and easy but with its depths, at once rational enough and endlessly resourceful in fancy.1

One interesting aspect of the Shingle Style that forms the beginnings of a possible rationale for its timelessness is the fact that the homes were designed to be uniquely responsive to the clients' personal needs. The spatial organization, informal spaces, orientation to celebrate views of the landscape, and innovative use of materials and details, coupled with the multiplicity of contextually evocative forms that clearly identified with the site, suggest the notion that these houses were sensitively designed to be responsive, distinctive, and personal. A second aspect worth noting is that these houses were designed to withstand the extremes of climate and variable weather conditions through the use of deep porches and overhangs for shading, carefully detailed exterior envelopes, and the heating/cooling of the interior. In short, this style reveals a true sensitivity to the realities of client needs, vernacular context, and environmental factors.

The writings of Vincent Scully acted as a catalyst for the first Shingle Style Revival period of the 1960s-70s. Although the architects utilized the original style's characteristics as a point of departure, they used a similar strategy of pluralistic experimentation. The works of Robert Venturi, Charles Moore, and Edward Larrabee Barnes, among numerous other architects, formed a body of work representative of this period, involving a reinterpretation and an abstraction of Shingle Style characteristics. A second wave of the Shingle Style revival occurred through the 1980s-90s. Although many of the architects from the first wave continued to design within this mode, many new faces joined the ranks including Turner Brooks, Steven Izenour, and Jeremiah Eck, among a multitude of others. As evidenced in the book Shingle Style Houses: Past and Present, and also in this sequel, it is apparent that a third wave of Shingle Style revival is alive and well with an ever-growing list of participating architects!

A close look at this present wave of twenty-first century Shingle Style revival shows an evolving body of work that continues the tradition of homes designed to be specifically responsive to the needs of the client. Clever, well-designed open and flowing spaces, circulation elements, the wide variations in spatial organization, and the informality of choreographed interior and exterior spaces, along with an ever-growing repertoire of new materials and building techniques, continue to reveal new possibilities. This creativity is even more evident today with the abundance of potential options, amenities, and technologies ranging from audio-visual computer systems, entertainment spaces, spas, and reading/meditation niches for mind and body, to radiant heated floors. Fine interior detailing is often observed. Although the interiors are contemporary, sometimes there are ties to the past through the occasional embracement of historical detailing.

The realities of rising energy costs, economic challenges, and increasing data regarding relationships connecting carbon emissions and climate change have effectively created a new mindset for sustainability. There is a desire on the part of the public for energy efficiency, renewable energy, and all things "green." The design of a sustainable home should intentionally result in a habitat that is durable, healthy, comfortable, energy efficient, and environmentally responsible. It is enlightening to realize that today's Shingle Style offers great potential for incorporating sustainable strategies. For example, the site can have indigenous landscaping with rainwater harvesting systems. The architect can select recyclable/renewable materials and preserve indoor air quality by using non-toxic carpets and paints with no Volatile Organic Compounds (VOCs). In addition, compact fluorescent lights offer high efficiency. Energy Star rated appliances and high efficiency plumbing fixtures can effectively reduce energy costs. Furthermore, the exterior envelope involves numerous component/type choices regarding cladding, windows, insulation, and moisture control, among other systems.

Sustainable strategies can also be applied to renovations and additions to existing homes. There are many old Shingle Style houses that can be modified and updated to accommodate twenty-first century lifestyles. Moreover, countless non-Shingle Style homes have the potential to be converted or transformed into a Shingle Style revival home. These types of projects allow for the re-use of existing buildings, giving new life to various degrees of existing concrete foundations, interior and exterior walls, and roof enclosures, as well as some of the interior finishes and woodwork. Although the magnitude of modifications can vary the amount of re-use of existing materials and systems, the important realization is that the final product often requires less energy to construct than a totally new building.

Renewable energy system options are also being incorporated. Innovative design can result in Shingle Style homes that optimize natural daylight and integrate passive solar design principles. Solar hot water systems can provide cost savings. Photovoltaic (PV) systems utilize the sun's perpetual energy to create electricity, thus reducing electric utility costs. In addition, wind systems utilize the wind's kinetic energy to supply electricity. These technologies are in a continual state of development, resulting in improved systems. Another efficient strategy involves geothermal heating and cooling systems, which utilize the Earth's natural heat, continuously supplied by the sun. These systems produce no on-site combustion of fossil fuels, with substantial savings in heating and cooling costs. Many of today's Shingle Style revival homes are now being designed with these alternative, renewable energy systems.

Although energy and environmental factors have certainly acquired importance in the present mode of design methodology, sustainable strategies can be planned and integrated with the fundamental characteristics of the Shingle Style, which are very much alive today. The present revival includes houses within the context of gardens, meadows, farmland, vineyards, forests, mountains and valleys, hillsides and bluffs, cliffs, waterfronts, harbors, as well as villages and urban settings. The sensitive juxtaposition of architecture and site, along with the hopes and dreams of the client are critical for a successful union. Furthermore, as demonstrated in the successful nineteenth century homes, today's carefully planned houses are also sited to celebrate views of the landscape. Indeed, the different orientations facing public streets, private yards, adjacent properties, distant vistas, as well as geographic and climatic factors offer cues for variations in facade design. In a sense, the architecture establishes a dialogue with the site context, offering the means to perceive and react with the outside world. Thus, the architects' imagination continues to create evocative forms that relate to the landscape, as well as to the local and regional vernacular context. The Shingle Style may be considered as an archetype that is reinterpreted, transformed, and abstracted through the interplay of geometry and form.

A sense of timelessness is inherent within the Shingle Style vernacular and within its revival manifestations, suggested by a lifespan stretching from the late nineteenth century through the early twenty-first century. The following paradigms are presented to summarize and articulate the rationale for this phenomenon:

- The notion of the picturesque house, expressed in a uniquely American style, offers a universal appeal.
- Well-designed, often informal spatial organization/circulation of interior spaces to accommodate living, leisure, entertainment, self-improvement, as well as work/study environments, along with evolving technologies, offers flexibility and perpetually new possibilities. The design process focuses on reacting to the client's needs and dreams in order to effectively result in creative and unique solutions.
- The sensitive juxtaposition of site and architecture effectively grounds the house for optimum use and placement with contextual relationships at multiple levels of meaning.
- The archetypal forms of the Shingle Style vernacular include a repertoire of undulating facades, capped with intersecting cross gable roof shapes, secondary hips, sheds, multi-form dormers, eyebrows, and curved sections, often with multi-level eaves, along with exterior shingle cladding. In addition, turrets, bays, balconies, porches, chimneys, as well as multiple window possibilities are included. This assemblage offers points of departure for pluralistic experimentation and the multiplicity of contextually evocative forms. Furthermore, there is limitless potential for reinterpretation, transformation, and abstraction through the interplay of geometry and form, as it relates to the local and regional vernacular context.
- A celebration of the landscape through the use of building orientation and the establishment of views accommodates the human appreciation for scenic beauty.
- The different orientations of the house facing public ways, private yard areas, distant vistas, as well as geographic and climatic factors offer cues for creative variations in the façade design. This responsive approach allows the house to establish a dialogue with the surrounding site, offering the means to perceive and react with the outside world.
- The use of porches and balconies, pushing and pulling on the building enclosure, offers multiple options for outside leisure as well as for the choreography of interior/exterior spatial interplay.
- A high-quality level of design and construction is often demonstrated by the interior detailing. The occasional embracement of historical themes within a contemporary context, offering ties to the past, can accommodate the human need for nostalgia.
- The growing and evolving selection of new, innovative materials and building techniques is a welcome palette for a style that has historically appreciated experimentation.
- The diversity in sustainable strategies, including energy efficient and environmentally sensitive systems and materials, renewable energy systems, as well as the re-use/modification of existing homes, is well-suited as an integral part of the design process. This responsive methodology is essential for an architecture that can hope to claim a sense of timelessness.

The integrated implementation of these paradigms suggests that Shingle Style homes of the twenty-first century are designed to be uniquely responsive to the users' personal needs and dreams, as well as to establish synergy with the site's vernacular context. Distinctive and personal, these houses are responsive with multiple levels of meaning as true expressions of a timeless architecture. In essence, this design methodology offers the potential for an architecture that is familiar yet new and refreshing, thus perpetually reinventing itself.

1 Vincent Scully excerpts taken from the introduction he wrote for The Architecture of the American Summer: The Flowering of the Shingle Style. Robert A.M. Stern, gen. ed. (Columbia University, New York, and Rizzoli International Publications, New York, 1989).

Acknowledgments

This book is a sequel to my 2007 *Shingle Style Houses: Past and Present*. My wonderful editor Tina Skinner convinced me that the time has come to revisit Shingle Style: perhaps because there has been so much feedback about the first book and because so many people are building in this style. Once again, Barbara Purchia has been a great friend and read over the manuscript.

Introduction

In the late 1800s, architects Henry Hobson Richardson, Charles McKim, and Stanford White began to revolt against the heavily ornate Victorian styles to experiment with shingle siding, and a style that was more American in feeling. For the next 20-30 years, Shingle Style spread throughout New England, became popular in the Mid-Atlantic, and migrated to California.

Named for that well-buttoned coat of shingles, the Shingle Style is free from the ornate details of earlier Victorian styles. Shingles have been substituted for corner boards and trim. From the way it faces the world to its oriels, turrets, wings, expansive spaces, and rough textures, the Shingle Style house is an integrated whole. Despite the fragmented massing, it has a sense of distinctiveness and timelessness with its well-proportioned spaces and good light.

Shingle Style was certainly influenced by the Gothic and Stick Styles, the Arts and Crafts movement, and Japanese art. Its practitioners, however, have a greater sense of continuity of surface and form and the connections among space. They opened up the interiors through porches, bays, and towers, covering the exterior forms with cedar shingles in various patterns. They designed central halls that were not just passageways but living spaces. They surrounded these halls with generous-sized rooms that permitted the sunlight to penetrate the depths of the house.

These houses were flexible—not self-consciously symmetrical as had been common in the past. Using pocket doors, the rooms flowed one to another. Inglenooks, bays, and alcoves allowed quieter activities. The owners reflected their interest in art and architecture in the quirks and details of fireplaces, spindles, balustrades, and other adornments such as their much loved beaded boarding.

Captains of industry and robber barons built these substantial mansions as shrines to their success. They employed craftsmen to carve the wood, to bend the copper, to cast the iron. With the onset of the Federal Income Tax and World War I, however, the fortunes of the wealthy disappeared. Labor costs escalated, and the style faded.

In the 1950s, the style came to the forefront again as a result of Yale architecture professor Vincent Scully's scholarly study. He coined the term Shingle Style to mean that subset of Queen Anne houses in which a uniform covering of shingles was used and which celebrated the informality of life at home. Once again, contemporary design began to be influenced by aspects of the Shingle Style—whether it was in the flexible handling of mass and space or in the use of shingles.

In the late 1800s, Caroline and Joseph Hodges Choate, a prominent New York attorney and U.S. Ambassador to the Court of St. James, decided to build a summer estate in the village of Stockbridge, Massachusetts. They selected a site on a narrow ledge that perched above a valley with a backdrop of dramatic hills. Designed by McKim, Mead & White in 1885 and completed in 1886, the Shingle Style Choate home belongs to a class of luxurious summer homes that are happily known as "summer cottages." Choate called it Naumkeag, the native name for his birthplace, Salem, Massachusetts. Mabel Choate, their second daughter, inherited the property in 1929. She and landscape architect Fletcher Steele concentrated on the gardens and the landscaped areas. When she died in 1958, she bequeathed Naumkeag and its contents to the Trustees of Reservations who continue to make the house and its gardens open to the public. *Courtesy of D. Peter Lund*

In the nineteenth century, Cape May was considered one of the finest seaside resorts in America. It is particularly significant for its large number of Queen Anne, Gothic revival, Shingle Style, and other Victorian structures. In 1976, the entire city was officially deigned a National Historic Landmark to ensure the architectural preservation of these buildings. *Courtesy of D. Peter Lund*

The Windward House, 1905, is a large Shingle Style Bed and Breakfast. It sports an intriguing array of window treatments. During restoration, workmen found the original shingles, still in good shape, under the asbestos siding, which was commonly used to update Victorian houses earlier in the twentieth century. *Courtesy of D. Peter Lund*

The massive Hotel Macomber, c. 1918, is a four-story example of Shingle Style. Today, it contains a hotel and shops. *Courtesy of D. Peter Lund*

The Humphrey Hughes House, 1913, has a grand veranda, which encircles three sides of the unpainted Shingle Style house. The house is named for Captain Humphrey Hughes who sailed to Cape May in 1660. *Courtesy of D. Peter Lund*

Toward the end of the twentieth century, homeowners again wanted that comfortable family look symbolized by the Shingle Style house. Increasingly, they turned to architects to design luxurious homes that capitalized on the skilled labor available to execute the exquisite details, including wide, overhanging front-facing gables or eyebrow-shaped windows. These homes have a power and grace born of basic materials and handcrafted details. Although many of these older homes were enormous—even by our modern-day standards—today's houses tend to be even grander. Great rooms or open plans that connect several spaces make sense in this dot com world where busy families have more to share and fit into their lives.

Often built to look like they've always been there, today's Shingle Style homes reflect the landscape and the history of the area. Thus, a new house in a small New England town may well reflect traditional New England vernacular and its Shingle Style precedents. The interior is more contemporary and casual, however. It is brighter, windows are more evident, and the exposed structure is highlighted with modern detailing. The stylistic reference is there in the shingles, in the flexibility of design, and in the broad sloping roof.

Today's shingles, like those of yesteryear, command the perfect view—whether it is undulating hills or the Atlantic. Sweeping windows and French doors draw in nature's panorama. Porches present a welcoming face to the public and blur the division between exterior and interior domains.

And again, a veritable army of gifted craftspeople with exquisite attention to detail customize these mansions for a contemporary lifestyle. Modern, energy-efficient windows in all shapes and sizes take in the view outside and even within. Towers add piquant notes to long silhouettes and provide new angles to familiar interior rooms. Theaters, home offices, wine cellars, alternative energy sources, health, safety, and security devices have major appeal. Walls are filled with modern technology connecting them to the outside world. Fine materials and beautifully designed and implemented spaces add to the livability and joy of the Shingle Style house.

In the last ten years, the Shingle Style has become increasingly popular. It has even appeared in nonresidential architecture. Its rough wooden shingles, the broad overhanging roof, and the wide shady porches encourage long lazy afternoons in rocking chairs. Spread low against the ground on heavy stone foundations, a Shingle Style home, with its long silver silhouette and irregular roofline looks more than capable of withstanding the test of time and weather.

Even the Shingle Style garage, with its integral overhang, that goes with this Shingle Style house is being insulated. *Courtesy of D. Peter Lund*

Built in 2007 on a busy suburban street, this forward-looking home used recycled materials, sustainably forested wood, and products with few or no volatile organic compounds. The energy-efficient home has an open floor plan. *Courtesy of D. Peter Lund*

Shingle Style houses and outbuildings are being built throughout suburbia today. *Courtesy of David S.R. Andreozzi and Brian Dougan*

Today's Shingles of Distinction

Roofs hovering over walls, spaces flowing into other spaces, dynamic lines and planes, the Shingle Style home gives us a sense of being home again. Today's shingles reflect their antecedents in the sunlit warmth of their casual asymmetrical layout, their graciously ascending stairways, the sturdiness of their strong lines punctuated by chimneys and towers, and custom designed details, moldings, and woodwork. In this section, we portray large (over 4,500 square feet) shingles built by today's architects. They reflect the tradition of the Shingle Style archetype, which can be seen in Naumkeag (see page 9), but have the amenities, technology, and convenience of the twenty-first century.

Ledges Residence

Designed by Gleysteen Design LLC, the house's form is long and narrow to work with its site. The building's massing consists of an organic composition of gables, bays, and a tower. A cupola acts as a light monitor into the family room on the end, and terraced patios extend the family living space outdoors. *Photo by Marcus Gleysteen*

A stone-lined streambed, with a boulder bridge, accommodates rainfall on its steep, rocky site. The stone is also integrated in the design of the terraced patios. *Photo by Marcus Gleysteen*

The house's overlapping forms add interest, depth, and beauty to the facade. A tower marks the main stairway, referencing the entry under the porch. *Photo by Marcus Gleysteen*

The stone patios and walkways link the house to its site. Building materials include painted shingle, stone, ornamental trim, and copper gutters and downspouts. Brackets under the overhangs and panels in the gables add scale. *Photo by Marcus Gleysteen*

A studied composition of gables at various scales frame the entry porch. *Photo by Marcus Gleysteen*

Ornamental brackets support the bay above the screen porch. The shallow bay window inset in the gable catches light, providing depth and interest. *Photo by Marcus Gleysteen*

Island House

Albert, Righter & Tittman designed a 5,000-square-foot Shingle Style vacation house in a historic island community off the Connecticut shore. This house anticipates the owners' transition into retirement and year-round use. The entry side is a picturesque composition of balanced asymmetry anchored by a conical tower. The round tower and gently flared gambrel roof give the sense of swelling volumes characteristic of the Shingle Style. *Courtesy of ChipRiegal.com*

The porch offers places to sit or dine, looking out over a golf course to the water. *Courtesy of ChipRiegal.com*

A band of windows wraps around the tower and onto the adjacent dormer, and the entry porch wraps around the base of the tower, bringing the elements together. The conical tower alludes to the French precedents that influenced the Shingle Style in its formative years. *Courtesy of ChipRiegal.com*

The capacious gambrel roof brings the eave line down low while accommodating three generous bedrooms on the second floor. At one end, a special pavilion houses a guest suite. *Courtesy of ChipRiegal.com*

The windows of the pointed, prow-like dormers are angled to take in a wide panoramic view. *Courtesy of ChipRiegal.com*

The main stairs wind upward through the conical tower and down into a generous entry hall, which leads to the living and dining rooms. *Courtesy of ChipRiegal.com*

A bookshelf-lined wall leads to the large, combined living and dining room facing the water. Substantial beams add texture to the ceiling. *Courtesy of ChipRiegal.com*

With a view to the water, the kitchen is an inviting space for family and guests to gather. *Courtesy of ChipRiegal.com*

A soft glow fills the porch for summer evening living. *Courtesy of ChipRiegal.com*

Balboa Beach Cottage

Originally built in the 1940s, this California Shingle Style beach cottage renovated by Brion Jeannette fronts directly on Newport Bay. The owners found the original house confined and dated; they wished to open the entire first level to make one "great room." Brion Jeannette also re-configured the upstairs bedrooms, bathrooms, and offices to provide more light and use the space more efficiently. *Courtesy of Jeffrey D. McCoy*

The architect also updated the patio. The new horizon edge swimming pool adjacent to the bulkhead provides an option for pool or beach play. This cottage will now be available for several more lifetimes. *Courtesy of Jeffrey D. McCoy*

Daisy Hill

Looking for a place of repose away from the corporate world, the clients desired a place that met the needs of their growing extended family. Working with Mark Chaney Architects, they generated an open plan that gave them centralized gathering spaces and room for older relatives to stay while permitting grandchildren to find hiding spaces and places to play. The home is located at the end of a long winding road at the crest of a hill. The lower level has a billiard room, wine cellar, gym, and spa/sauna. The main level includes the kitchen, dining room, great room, reading room, a guest bedroom, and the master bedroom suite. The upper level provides a guest bedroom, office, and bathrooms. The surrounding site provides sunlight and a walking trail through the woods. Daisy Hill is a gathering spot for friends and family during every season of the year. *Courtesy of Mark Chaney Photography*

The five-bay garage wing connects to a mudroom. Driving surfaces are light in color and pervious to reduce water runoff. The mud room, laundry room, and "rover room" for the dog separate the garage from the main house, eliminating the flow of unwanted or toxic fumes into the air supply for the main house. *Courtesy of Mark Chaney Photography*

A variety of openings on to exterior decks and terraces provides connections to the natural surroundings. Here, the second level office balcony extends over a breakfast room. *Courtesy of Mark Chaney Photography*

The main level kitchen facade setbacks help delineate the two-story exterior envelope. Decorative shingles wrap continuously around the two-story space pulling the facade together, while the subtle angle in the walls brings a special touch to both exterior and interior. In the kitchen, the angle provides space between the sink and wall for both aesthetic and functional needs. On the upper level, a home office is defined with high ceilings and a vertical wall angle. *Courtesy of Mark Chaney Photography*

Daisy Hill is a combination of recyclable natural materials including wood, stone, steel, glass, and concrete. The home exterior is predominately a red cedar shingle siding, with a fieldstone base, and cedar shake roof. The smart home system throughout controls lighting and HVAC zones. There is a high efficiency furnace and air conditioning system. An alternative fuel source, wood for the present, provides a reduced dependency on oil. *Courtesy of Mark Chaney Photography*

The dining room looks towards the front entry. Daylight floods the home through operable windows. Very few volatile organic compounds were used in the construction process. *Courtesy of Mark Chaney Photography*

The kitchen includes Energy Star appliances, recyclable granite counters, and oak floors. The cabinets are made of heart grain pine reclaimed from the beams of an old mill building. *Courtesy of Mark Chaney Photography*

The kitchen desk is adjacent to the cylindrical breakfast room with the great room beyond. *Courtesy of Mark Chaney Photography*

The wet bar in the great room mirrors the grand fieldstone fireplace at the far end. *Courtesy of Mark Chaney Photography*

Scissor truss beams provide both structural support and repetitive rhythm across the ceiling while French doors open out onto a stone terrace. The cedar trellis over the terrace shades the great room from hot summer sunlight. *Courtesy of Mark Chaney Photography*

Eel Point

This 15,000-square-foot Shingle Style home, designed by Nantucket Architecture Group, Ltd. , overlooks Nantucket Sound. The property has a 4,800-square-foot guesthouse, a swimming pool, a 60 x 120 foot sports court, and extensive landscaping. *Courtesy of Jeffrey Allen*

Shingle details. *Courtesy of Jeffrey Allen*

The children's deck roof has all cedar trim. *Courtesy of Jeffrey Allen*

The main staircase is a delight.
Courtesy of Jeffrey Allen

The main house incorporates a reclaimed barn frame as the main living space and is filled with activity spaces for arts and crafts, exercise, and family movie going. The bedrooms have balconies located off of gathering spaces. *Courtesy of Jeffrey Allen*

THE FOURTH WAR

Large windows allow for light-filled spaces with generous views. The stairs are a pronounced image in the house. *Courtesy of Jeffrey Allen*

The 11,000 Square Foot Estate

Designed in 2003 by Living Spaces Architectural Associates, this estate represents the sophistication of the vintage Shingle Style homes of the past. This house has Victorian overtones with the positioning of an octagon tower in the front. It has a cedar roof and siding with "woven" corners and flares overhanging a massive fieldstone foundation. The use of gambrel roof lines, large stone chimneys, and accents of scalloped shingles complete the exterior. *Courtesy of the Architect*

To blend in with the community, the architect gave this large home a modest sized look on the front exterior. In true Shingle Style planning, the 11,000-square-foot house takes full advantage of its location on a river. As the river winds, so does the house to optimize and differentiate the views as seen from the various rooms. *© Dan Gair/Blind Dog Photo, Inc.*

Drawing its influences from the gatehouse of the past, the detached carriage house was added in 2007. The traditional wood doors accent the use of stone with cedar-flared siding. Decorative wood brackets support the sweeping cedar roof. Inside the carriage house is Douglas fir beadboard wood interior. On the second floor is a caretaker's apartment featuring an opening kitchen, dining and living area with a bedroom and bath. © *Dan Gair/Blind Dog Photo, Inc.*

The main house is entered through a rounded porch supported by large columns. An oversized elaborate mahogany front door leads into a 12-foot wide center hall that extends from front to back, where it exits onto a rounded screen porch. The hall is comprised of a colonnade of arches and columns. On one side is a formal library with cherry wood paneling and detailing. © *Dan Gair/Blind Dog Photo, Inc.*

On the other side is a large dining room with an oval backlit coffered ceiling. © *Dan Gair/Blind Dog Photo, Inc.*

On the lower level is a lounge reminiscent of the fine entertaining parlors of the past. A wide curved stair takes one into this extraordinary room with its10-foot, paneled ceiling. A full size bar with a wine cellar is on one end; the eight-foot high French doors open onto a back patio. A swimming pool with an Oriental influenced cabana is connected to this patio. © *Dan Gair/Blind Dog Photo, Inc.*

Hidden Hill

Designed by Robert Storm Architects, the 6,500-square-foot house is just a short drive up a narrow curving road from the town's busy beachfront neighborhood—but a world away. Flared at the end, the swooping front gable and porch create an inviting entry. *Courtesy Mark Samu—Samu Studios, Inc.*

The site, tight in the front, dictated the compact L-shape plan. The asymmetrical facade, stair tower, and eyebrow window are distinctive to Shingle Style design. *Courtesy Mark Samu—Samu Studios, Inc.*

The light pastel color palate of the first floor and the weathered, white oak floors add to the home's seaside character. The large foyer is flooded with light from the window dominating the traditional paneled stair tower and French doors in the adjacent great room. Inside, the house features a large central open area across the back with a great room, breakfast area, kitchen, and children's play area. *Courtesy Mark Samu—Samu Studios, Inc.*

Unique to the house, and strategically positioned near the garage, is a small chart/fishing room, where the owner can store his gear and plan his next deep-sea adventure. The theme is even carried through to the wall treatment. *Courtesy Mark Samu—Samu Studios, Inc.*

Casual, uncluttered furnishings make this traditional home comfortable for a young family. *Courtesy Mark Samu—Samu Studios, Inc.*

Lots of built-in storage and closet space throughout the house keep an active family organized. A mirror reflects a portion of the master closet. Built-in storage here and in other parts of the house creates the "no clutter" simplicity the couple prefers. *Courtesy Mark Samu—Samu Studios, Inc.*

The large open kitchen, combined with the great room, is the central gathering place for the family. With French doors along one wall, the sunny space has easy access to the terrace, pool, and backyard play areas. *Courtesy Mark Samu—Samu Studios, Inc.*

The white on white of the custom cabinetry is a classic touch for the seaside house. *Courtesy Mark Samu—Samu Studios, Inc.*

A wide hallway on the second floor connects a master suite, the children's bedrooms (each with its own bath), and a playroom. At the rear, second and third floor balconies allow for panoramic views of the sound. *Courtesy Mark Samu—Samu Studios, Inc.*

Reflecting details from the house, the pool house is a miniature Shingle Style folly. *Courtesy Mark Samu—Samu Studios, Inc.*

Silver Twig

R.S. Granoff Architects P.C. designed this 6,500- square-foot house as a family retreat where the clients could relax, entertain, and spend the summer with their children. The front porch and porte cochere create an inviting look to this Shingle Style farmhouse. *Courtesy of Elliott Kaufman*

This home design won first place in *Architectural Digest*'s New York 2008 open audition. *Courtesy of Elliott Kaufman*

Gable roofs, towers, expansive overhangs, brackets, shingle siding, and asymmetrical composition are signature elements. *Courtesy of Elliott Kaufman*

The dramatic one and half story great room has a large picture window facing the back yard and trusses made of dark antique wood beams. *Courtesy of Elliott Kaufman*

The light-filled stair tower with Shaker paneling provides a strong architectural and visual element. *Courtesy of Elliott Kaufman*

To celebrate the owners' extensive art collection, special display walls were built for flat art, while customized "art nooks" house specific sculptures. *Courtesy of Elliott Kaufman*

Exposed beams of reclaimed wood punctuate the ceiling of the large country kitchen with its brick hearth and white cabinets. *Courtesy of Elliott Kaufman*

What began as a bonus room above the garage became a bright and cheerful teen lounge. Light comes in from windows on three sides and the cupola. *Courtesy of Elliott Kaufman*

The master bedroom with white paneled cathedral ceiling and dark, wood furniture has a relaxed airy feeling. *Courtesy of Elliott Kaufman*

The house has terraces on the first and second floors overlooking the backyard. Doors open to a pool patio. Porch columns with latticed brackets, gable ends with board and batten siding, and diamond-shaped windows are unique features. *Courtesy of Elliott Kaufman*

Cape Tower

Designed by Albert, Righter & Tittman, this seaside vacation house is an essay on the imagery of New England shingled resort architecture. It belongs to a private association of homes occupying a small island. The approach to the house centers on the stair tower, the main vertical element in an otherwise horizontal composition. The tower, together with matching cupolas on the garage and guest bedroom wing, establishes symmetry. The off-center front door, and other asymmetrical elements relax the formality. *Courtesy of © Robert Benson Photography*

The arrival courtyard is a sheltered, sunny spot with a grid of garden beds. The flared profile of the stair tower is reminiscent of old lighthouses. Beyond, the guest bedroom hall has a jaunty alternating rhythm of windows. *Courtesy of © Robert Benson Photography*

The living room chimney, like that of the family room at the opposite end of the house, threads through the second floor gable and reappears above the roof. Boldly scaled decorative brackets visually support the big overhang around the chimneys, although the exterior painted trim is, for the most part, kept simple. *Courtesy of © Robert Benson Photography*

The main part of the house is a long, thin bar, giving water views both to ground floor living rooms and to family bedrooms above. The small seaside community strongly encouraged new houses to keep a low profile. A gambrel roof brings the eaves down low while accommodating four bedrooms on the second floor. *Courtesy of © Robert Benson Photography*

The long porch offers places to sit or dine overlooking the water. *Courtesy of © Robert Benson Photography*

The living room is a light-colored counterpart to the same-size wood-paneled family room at the opposite end of the house. Wicker furniture, a summerhouse staple, is reinterpreted in unexpected bright colors. *Courtesy of © Robert Benson Photography*

Between the dining room and family room, the kitchen is the heart of the house, opening up onto a waterside porch. A sitting area in the bay window and an informal eating area make the kitchen a gathering place. *Courtesy of © Robert Benson Photography*

The painted horizontal board wainscoting helps organize the hallway. A built-in seat in an alcove helps expand the sense of space and provides a convenient perch to take off your boots. *Courtesy of © Robert Benson Photography*

Windows on three sides bring in southern light while also opening up to northern water views. The natural wood paneling complements the light paint colors throughout the rest of the house. The Delft tile fireplace surround provides further seaside imagery. *Courtesy of © Robert Benson Photography*

The Tower House

Living Spaces Architectural Associates designed the Tower House, seen here in an aerial view, which was built on a site that previously was a US Coast Guard Station. In 1967, the military building was renovated and became a contemporary piece of architectural sculpture. A five-sided, 52-foot tower and a 45-foot "flying roof deck" were added, creating the drama that make this structure a landmark on the New Hampshire coast. Under new ownership, the old structure was demolished, and a 5,100-square-foot contemporary Shingle Style home was designed, keeping the elements that created the "landmark" drama. *Courtesy of Veodao Nu Bunnag*

The new design turned the house 45 degrees, giving greater views. Fitting the "site specific" design on one-third acre and meeting all the environmental and town setback requirements also created the "shape" of the house's footprint. *Courtesy of Veodao Nu Bunnag*

The visual play of the different modules of the house accentuates the tower and flying roof deck, which is supported by a steel frame. *Courtesy of Veodao Nu Bunnag*

Multiple roof lines converge at the chimney. There are no flat roofs, and extra care was taken to build a "weather proof" house to withstand the extreme climate of this location. The contemporary styling includes traditional use of roof overhangs, windows, exterior trim, and siding—elements of a Shingle Style home of the past reinvented for the future. *Courtesy of Veodao Nu Bunnag*

The frame of the house was a collaboration of wood and steel framing. A gymnastic connection is made between the tower and the private roof deck. Steel posts with curved brackets are supporting members. *Courtesy of Veodao Nu Bunnag*

The first floor contains the four-car garage, the main storage area, a seasonal entertainment cabana, and the main foyer. A contemporary stair goes from the first floor foyer to the second floor. An elevator takes you to the second and third floors. On the second floor, a kitchenette and lounge provide a separate environment for the four complete guest bedroom suites. In this upside down house, the third floor is the main level. This is where the open kitchen, dining, and living areas experience the magnificent view. The master bedroom suite and home office are also on the third floor. Every room in the house has an ocean view. Above the third floor is the "flying roof deck" and signature tower. *Courtesy of Veodao Nu Bunnag*

The interior is finished in a contemporary way. The living room has a contemporary fireplace and a cathedral ceiling. The kitchen has flush mahogany cabinets giving it a nautical feel. The dining area has a coffered gilded ceiling that reflects the light of the panoramic windows. *Courtesy of Veodao Nu Bunnag*

Carmel House

The site strongly influenced the design of this California shingle by Gleysteen Design. In this view from the rear, the house sits among the mature trees and a rolling hill. *Photo by Marcus Gleysteen*

The exterior details consist of lookout-beam expressions, curving dormers, and natural wood soffits. There is a view axis from the front entry through the rear entry to a live oak in the back yard. *Photo by Marcus Gleysteen*

The end gable of the family room is a composition of glass with butt-glazed corners. The reading nook bumps out under an extended eave, and the rear entry aligns with the live oak. *Photo by Marcus Gleysteen*

The informal dining area, open to the family room, has a pair of French doors leading to the patio. The formal living and dining room also look out to this outdoor space.

The rear entry looks through the hallway, open between the formal living and dining rooms, to the main front entry. *Photo by Marcus Gleysteen*

The family room reading nook has 180-degree views of the backyard and the view beyond. *Photo by Marcus Gleysteen*

The outdoor fireplace is set into the slope. *Photo by Marcus Gleysteen*

The hallway is open, with columns to both the dining room and living rooms. *Photo by Marcus Gleysteen*

The stone family room fireplace and wood ceiling link the outdoors to the interior. A ridge skylight highlights the space. *Photo by Marcus Gleysteen*

The family room reading nook is a special place to view the house and its site. *Photo by Marcus Gleysteen*

Historic District Shingle

This new Shingle Style home designed by Nantucket Architecture Group Ltd. needed to meet strict historic district guidelines. *Courtesy of Jeffrey Allen*

Its low roof lines minimize the visual impact of this 8,400-square-foot home. The abundant native landscaping ensures privacy for family activities. *Courtesy of Jeffrey Allen*

The gracious entry hall has a beautifully carved period stairway. *Courtesy of Jeffrey Allen*

The entry hall reflects its historic precedents with other rooms flowing into it. *Courtesy of Jeffrey Allen*

The family room has a massive fireplace and reclaimed church paneling. *Courtesy of Jeffrey Allen*

The expansive kitchen is bright with natural lighting. *Courtesy of Jeffrey Allen*

The children's bathroom allows for washing and splashing. *Courtesy of Jeffrey Allen*

The master bath and massage room. *Courtesy of Jeffrey Allen*

Even the dogs have their own shower here! *Courtesy of Jeffrey Allen*

Fusion: Modern Shingle Style and Lakefront Vernacular

George Fellner of Fellner Associates Architects designed this Connecticut lakefront house as a major transformation/expansion, connecting two existing structures with a new infill space and adding a new second floor. The west facade seen here reveals an assemblage of irregular and asymmetrical forms. The roof displays intersecting main cross gables, hips, sheds, secondary gables, and multi-level eaves. Acting as a pivotal focal point, the primary octagonal tower of the kitchen is integrated into the main volume. The arched entry with stone steps offers an inviting introduction to the home. All in all, the numerous connotative references suggest a modern interpretation of the Shingle Style. *Courtesy of George Fellner*

Interested in a maintenance-free exterior, the clients selected a textured, irregular vinyl siding for the main upper walls. Considering its durability and recyclable benefits, this material turned out to be a reasonable choice. A stone finish was used on the base surfaces, tower elements, chimney, and at the arched entry to complement the shingle siding aesthetic. Composed of lightweight concrete formed in molds using recycled fly ash, this sustainable system is one-quarter the weight of regular stone. This secondary abstracted octagonal tower of the master bathroom acts as a counterpoint to the main tower, providing asymmetrical balance. The playful windows are whimsically placed, evoking eyes, nose, and mouth elements. *Courtesy of George Fellner*

As viewed from the lake, the home's east facade evokes a lakefront vernacular theme that celebrates leisure and recreation. An array of insulated windows with low-emittance (low-E) glazing leads to extensive exterior multi-level decks, establishes a personal dialogue with the lake, and provides natural daylight and ventilation. A new patio of pervious stone pavers allows for natural storm water management, reducing runoff. *Courtesy of George Fellner*

Wrap-around, multi-level decks offer multiple areas for outside lounging and recreation. The use of horizontal rows of metal cables in the railing system allows for nearly transparent views of the lake, which contributes towards the lakefront vernacular image with nautical overtones. Composed of a wood-plastic composite, the decking makes use of reclaimed wood from the woodworking industry and recycled plastic. *Courtesy of George Fellner*

The original one-story house and separate garage with a second-floor apartment served as a starting point. Using a sustainable strategy focusing on reusable materials, only 10 percent of the concrete foundation was newly poured. Instead, the house was efficiently constructed by re-using the existing concrete foundation, exterior walls, and 35 percent of the existing interior walls. With an open plan for living, cooking, and dining areas along with the master bedroom suite, the new second-floor structure is composed of a newly engineered lumber system of I-joists made from fast growing, small diameter trees. A hydro-air system heats and cools six zones throughout the house for optimum efficiency and comfort control. *Courtesy of George Fellner*

The octagonal kitchen opens directly to the living/dining area. As a telescopic form, the upper roof steps inward and is perforated with clerestory windows, benefiting the kitchen with cascading daylight. The copper finish on the ceiling surfaces makes a subliminal reference to cookware. *Courtesy of George Fellner*

The master bedroom suite consists of study with his and hers computer area, as well as the sleeping area. A high ceiling provides the opportunity for a spiral stair leading to a reading loft with its own exterior deck. The remodeled first floor accommodates a series of bedrooms, bathrooms, den, laundry, storage, and mechanical spaces. The space over the garage serves as a guest suite, and a series of recreation and lounge areas are in the new connecting infill spaces. Although the total area is 5,900 sq. ft., 50 percent of the space is dedicated to multiple guest suite use. *Courtesy of George Fellner*

East Chop West

The clients' passion for their New England, East Chop Cape Cod home influenced Brion Jeanette's design of "East Chop West" in a private community in California. Perched on the corner of a generous tree-lined parcel, this beautiful family home reflects many nuances of classical shingle architecture. *Courtesy of EricFigge.com*

The home wraps around a large, central outdoor family room with garden, pool, pool house, entertainment, and guest quarters, creating a generous outdoor environment that is enjoyed from the interior living space. *Courtesy of EricFigge.com*

The parlor/sitting room off the main entry provides visitors with a warm welcome. For a busy family of five, this room provides a quiet respite that is enjoyed by friends and family who seek an out-of-the-way spot for a visit or somewhere to catch up on the day's events. *Courtesy of Jeffrey D. McCoy*

The kitchen opens wide on each end to incorporate the outside. Architects Brion Jeannette and Amy Creager designed this kitchen for ease, function, and group activities—from prep to presentation. *Courtesy of Jeffrey D. McCoy*

This pool house doubles as a guest-house. Whether it's a slumber party, visiting in-laws, or a 4th of July barbecue, this pool house can handle it all. It welcomes parties of all sizes and easily converts to overnight quarters for guests that can't bring themselves to leave. Designed as a stand-alone structure in the backyard, it opens freely to a cozy outdoor fireplace and the sparkling pool area. *Courtesy of Jeffrey D. McCoy*

"Gracious" is the immediate emotion evoked by this view of the house from the expansive play and pool area. Each room embraces the outdoor space, shutting out the world and focusing only on relaxing and pleasure. *Courtesy of Jeffrey D. McCoy*

Clapboard Hill Colonial Revival

Symmetry is the hallmark of this grand, 7,000 -square-foot home created by Robert Storm Architects. A long, imposing driveway draws the eye to the matching windows and roof peaks on either side of the entry. Once inside, opposing fireplaces in the dining and living room accentuate the symmetrical nature of these formal spaces in the front of the house. *Courtesy of the Architect*

The family room opens to the eat-in kitchen where a wine refrigerator and storage cabinet is convenient to both rooms. Besides the built-in cabinetry, the room has a large fireplace and French doors leading to the patio and pool. *Courtesy of the Architect*

Flooded with light from its south-facing windows, the living room's tray ceiling adds to the formality. *Courtesy of the Architect*

The oak library with windows on three sides has become an elegant home office. A door to the patio provides easy access to the outside. *Courtesy of the Architect*

The large kitchen is divided into several areas, which works equally well for one cook or caterers for a large party. The service area consists of a laundry, a mudroom with a dog washing area, and storage for the family. *Courtesy of the Architect*

The architect originally envisioned this space, which is part of the master suite, as an office or exercise room. The room is now decorated as a sitting area. *Courtesy of the Architect*

On the second floor there is a master suite, with a sitting room, a bath, closets, and an outdoor balcony, as well as five other bedrooms, each with its own bath. Simplicity and a neutral palate make the airy master bedroom a comforting oasis. *Courtesy of the Architect*

The master bath features a steam shower and a large whirlpool tub. Classic white marble and a fireplace create a calm spa quality to the room. *Courtesy of the Architect*

Large Summer Cottage

David Andreozzi was asked to design an updated version of a summer home with the true spirit of a nineteenth century Shingle Style summer cottage. The vacation home is located on four open acres of land. Its gambrel roofs and deeply profiled moldings are intended to let the primary visual experience be the different level of light that dances on the various planes of the woven shingles. State of the art technology separates the old historic archetype from the new, including engineered hurricane wind loading design, a vertical closed loop geothermal HVAC system, and a complicated insulation design including icynene insulation in the roof with a heat recovery ventilator that supplies outside air to compensate for the tight construction of the house. *Courtesy of Aaron Usher III*

The symmetry about the front door and the stone chimneys is designed to appear strong enough to bond the residence to its site but also remain informal enough to welcome friends in flip-flops. *Courtesy of Aaron Usher III*

At eighty-three feet above sea level, the essence of the design becomes evident: it's about the myriad ocean views from each room on the east side of the house. *Courtesy of Aaron Usher III*

A simply designed swimming pool bonds the main house to a carriage house with a second level guest suite. *Courtesy of Aaron Usher III*

The main living room features a custom-designed mantle, woodwork, coffered ceiling, and oversized French doors with diamond transoms. *Courtesy of Aaron Usher III*

A custom-designed kitchen acts as command central for the family room with a view to the pool and the ocean to the east. *Courtesy of Aaron Usher III*

The front entry's clerestory and the one-story wainscoting provide welcoming warmth upon entering the house. *Courtesy of Aaron Usher III*

A library/study has a custom mantle with soapstone hearth and surrounds, and a herringbone firebox. The matching hidden double doors connect to the living room with views to the kitchen beyond. *Courtesy of Aaron Usher III*

Highland Residence

Mitchell Wilk Architecture believes that the allure of the Shingle Style is the ability to play with various forms and shapes, in both plan and elevation. In some architectural styles, these forms and elements juxtaposed against each other can create "aesthetic chaos." In this style, the shingle material itself is a unifying force, helping to mesh the disparate elements together into a cohesive design. Here, multiple gables, layered architectural forms, sweeping eave lines, and a separate garage wing create visual interest while maintaining a residential scale that is in keeping with the homes in the neighborhood. *Courtesy of Douglas Wilk*

Ample roof overhangs with brackets, layered architectural elements, and sweeping shingled walls create a shadow play across the front facade. Pressure-treated red cedar shingles are used. *Courtesy of Douglas Wilk*

The outer walls of the kitchen, with their muted off-white cabinetry, honed marble counter tops, and marble mosaic wall are in direct contrast to the dark stained island; granite counter; and random width, wide plank walnut flooring. *Courtesy of Douglas Wilk*

The family room is the central gathering spot in this home. Its freestanding stone structure creates a visual anchor. It houses the fireplace and audio/visual center on the front, with log storage, bookshelves and game storage on the backside. *Courtesy of Douglas Wilk*

The kitchen and informal dining area create a unified space, extending from the windows at the sink, overlooking the front yard, to the bay window of the dining area, looking out towards the rear yard. *Courtesy of Douglas Wilk*

The custom patina copper exhaust hood acts as the visual counterpoint to the subtle marble mosaic wall and floating shelves. *Courtesy of Douglas Wilk*

An Architect's Home

Designed and built by Living Spaces Architectural Associates, this 5,400-square-foot residence was built in 2004. Situated on six acres of woodland, the building site overlooks a saltwater estuary that feeds into the ocean. The house is oriented to take full advantage of the "sunset over the water" with its westerly exposure. The yellow colored siding and the emerald green heavy textured roof are both Victorian in nature. *Courtesy of Veodao Nu Bunnag*

The Shingle Style exterior is complimented by color and detail. There is a whimsical mix of Victorian, English, and Asian elements in this house. The square tower brings in the Victorian quality to the front while the "English Garden" element of the front porch with the white lattice placed between the columns connects the lavish gardens and landscaping. *Courtesy of Veodao Nu Bunnag*

There is a Chinese moon gate entry porch into the lower level space, a curved Balinese roof line peak in several areas, and an authentic Balinese gazebo in the back yard. One of the most important attributes of the modern Shingle Style movement is its ability to be eclectic. Many influences can shape these houses. They can also be asymmetrical, arty, and colorful. Shingle Style homes are inherently green and organic. *Courtesy of Veodao Nu Bunnag*

The interior trim is a mix with Victorian rope casings, Georgian crown moldings, and Balinese chair rail. Saturated greens and reds are in the coloration of the walls. The spacious living room with large windows has a fireplace with an ornate carved wood surround from India. It was a headboard to a bed that was retro-fitted to become a mantle for the fireplace. *Courtesy of Veodao Nu Bunnag*

The grand foyer has a curving mahogany stairway with carved wood balusters and the view that goes all the way through to the water. *Courtesy of Veodao Nu Bunnag*

An octagon formal dining room is accented with a custom, hand carved dining room set made especially for the house. *Courtesy of Veodao Nu Bunnag*

Through an arched opening, one enters the unique kitchen. The custom-designed, hand carved teak cabinet doors were made in Bali and shipped for installation. *Courtesy of Veodao Nu Bunnag*

The all-wood post and beam screened porch invites one to sit and contemplate the serene view.

Deerpath Estate

The entrance court to this imposing residence, designed by Gleysteen Design LLC, leads beyond the house to an additional parking court. The front elevation has a picturesque and organic approach to the building's massing, while integrating a fully contemporary interior layout. *Photo by Marcus Gleysteen*

A large, asymmetrical gable organizes the main facade. The strong resulting diagonals visually link the house to the landscape. Stonewalls also tie the house to the ground and extend into the gardens beyond. *Photo by Marcus Gleysteen*

The elegantly detailed shingle, slate, and stone-clad house belies the true nature of its steel and concrete frame. *Photo by Marcus Gleysteen*

Solid timber brackets, carrying the bay above, rest on granite buttresses. A hand forged bronze grill embellishes the glazed front door and sidelights. *Photo by Marcus Gleysteen*

The primary garage doors face an interior courtyard and are not visible from the street. A bridge links the main house to the carriage house. It also shelters the door to the mudroom below. *Photo by Marcus Gleysteen*

A peek-a-boo chimney with articulated stone work anchors the end elevation of the house.
Photo by Marcus Gleysteen

The family room is organized around the view, the fireplace, and a TV. An oak timber frame supports the foam-insulated roof and walls and articulates the Venetian plaster ceiling. *Photo by Marcus Gleysteen*

The main stair is detailed in quarter-sawn oak. The hand forged bronze balusters create a repeating pattern moving up the staircase. *Photo by Marcus Gleysteen*

RockSyde

Designed by Albert, Righter & Tittman, this 5,000-square-foot Shingle Style house is sited on a rocky shoulder of land. The garage and two low wings of the house define the intimate courtyard. There are no clues indicating the size of the house. *Courtesy of © Robert Benson Photography*

Although low and intimate on the uphill west and south sides, the house reveals a grander presence on the downhill north side as it sails out towards the ocean. The stone base keeps it rooted in the landscape. *Courtesy of © Robert Benson Photography*

A sunny, sheltered outdoor living space with an ocean view occupies an area defined by the long, meandering south side of the house on one side and the natural rock outcropping on the other. The small-scaled pavilion-like domed study punctuates the south facade. *Courtesy of © Robert Benson Photography*

Rocksyde abuts the former site of the historic (1887) Shingle Style, Kragsyde, by Peabody & Stearns. The stone base, great arch, and geometric complexity pay homage to that long-gone famous neighbor. The brown shingles and dark green trim also embrace Shingle Style traditions. *Courtesy of © Robert Benson Photography*

The east end is like a prow, with an enormous triple-hung window overlooking the sea. *Courtesy of © Robert Benson Photography*

The entry is a rotunda with a ceiling of ornamental ribs suggesting a dome. The rotunda cleverly shifts the axis from the front door to the rooms beyond. The walls are white, painted wood bands, giving the impression of masonry rustication. *Courtesy of © Robert Benson Photography*

The stacked black and white steps appear to be suspended in mid-air in front of a huge window. *Courtesy of © Robert Benson Photography*

An enormous triple-hung window frames the ocean view. *Courtesy of © Robert Benson Photography*

A decorative frieze with patterns of intersecting circles alternating with vertical lines wraps the dining room. The frieze becomes part of a screen of columns as it passes across the stair, separating the two spaces but allowing the light to stream through from the window beyond. *Courtesy of © Robert Benson Photography*

A classically detailed opening in a wall of books leads to an inviting alcove with window seat. *Courtesy of © Robert Benson Photography*

Shingles of Note

Despite its seeming simplicity, a Shingle Style house offers fine design details and craftsmanship. Towers, encircling porches, balconies, bay windows, large vestibules, elaborate fireplaces—even medium-size Shingle Style homes offer luxurious notes.

The Woodland House

After several years of living on the East Coast, and missing their West Coast Shingle Style house, the clients requested Architect André G. Fontaine to design a new house for them. The completed 3,000-square-foot house is sited below the crest of a hill overlooking the stream valley with its major rooms oriented to the south. The exterior features a dramatic chimney and a two-story box bay, as well as a south-facing screen porch and a roof top deck for the master bedroom. The living room is on the left with its grand chimney and two-story box bay. *Courtesy of Erik Kvalsvik*

The two-story living room occupies the entire southwest wing of the house. *Courtesy of Erik Kvalsvik*

The chimney is stucco-covered masonry. The shingles have a dark stain, and the trim is stained a dark green. *Courtesy of Erik Kvalsvik*

This detail view of the living room side of the stair wall shows acid-etched pewter panels separated by naturally finished oak strips. All of the horizontal surfaces have oak caps. The zigzag at the top right is the ceiling of the second floor hall bridge. *Courtesy of Erik Kvalsvik*

In this view of the stairs and entry hall, the dining room is on the right. The interiors of the main rooms are trimmed in naturally finished oak. Many of the light fixtures were designed by the architect and fabricated by the client. Note the zigzag wall of the second floor hall bridge, which is carried through to the master bedroom balcony overlooking the living room. *Courtesy of Erik Kvalsvik*

The two-story living room has a window seat overlooking the valley, an energy-saving fireplace, and windows on three walls. *Courtesy of Erik Kvalsvik*

This view of the living room is from the entry hall. The zigzag ceiling is the second floor hall bridge. *Courtesy of Erik Kvalsvik*

The dining room is several steps up from this room, allowing it to share the fireplace and the views beyond. The exposed, painted, rough cut lumber and wood decking impart a rustic quality and more interest to the ceiling. *Courtesy of Erik Kvalsvik*

The buffet in the dining room has an acid-etched pewter inlay in the counter and the cabinet doors. Note the exposed framing and wood decking at the ceiling. The living room fireplace and window seat are visible beyond. *Courtesy of Erik Kvalsvik*

The kitchen and breakfast room on the southeast corner are well placed to allow for early morning sun. The second floor master suite is located on this corner as well. The secondary bedrooms, the garage, and other services are located on the north side of the house providing a buffer from the winter weather. *Courtesy of Erik Kvalsvik*

The Shingle Cottage

Living Spaces Architectural Associates designed this waterfront Shingle Style home. The half-acre lot is triangular in shape, with the ocean in the front and a salt marsh behind it. Architect Ralf Amsden created an angled design where the footprint of the house was maximized within the lot, right up to each setback. Even a two-car garage was made to fit. By positioning the room zoning properly, every room in the house has one of the three water views. The modulation of the home is based on a gambrel roof line with hip roof extensions. An octagonal tower opens up the view in the front. The exterior design employs the classic Shingle Style materials. The foundation is fieldstone with flood louvers installed to allow water to move under the house in the event of a storm. The walls are shingled with "woven" corners and flairs. The walls and roof have a waterproof membrane underneath because of the extreme ocean exposure. In addition, the entire frame of the house is insulated with waterproof urethane foam so there is no need for venting the roof. Any vent in this location could leak. The roof has a 50-year guarantee asphalt shingle needed for wind protection. *Courtesy of John Hession*

The foyer has an interior stone-lined wall and a graceful stairway with graduated steps. There is also an elevator in this house. No longer a cost item, elevators provide full access to the house. *Courtesy of John Hession*

A formal fireplace accents the open concept kitchen, dining, and living area. The view through the living room and dining area continues out to the ocean. Large French doors open onto a "sea porch," a curvilinear space with columns. On the back of the house is a glass porch called the sunset room, as it looks over the salt marsh and toward the setting sun. *Courtesy of John Hession*

The second floor master bedroom features a special "domed" ceiling, fireplace, and deck beyond the French doors. *Courtesy of John Hession*

A mahogany paneled den is a special place to work while watching the boats in the harbor. *Courtesy of John Hession*

New England Mountain House

Set on a stone plinth, this house designed by Albert, Righter & Tittman nestles into a shoulder of the hill, high enough to get a commanding view but staying well below the tree line of the hilltop. The land falls away from the house site to the west, leaving clear, unobstructed views of a nearby lake. The house picks up on the spirit of an old rustic octagonal sleeping pavilion that had long existed on the hillside below. *Courtesy of © Robert Benson Photography*

The sweeping, all-encompassing hipped roof flares out at the eave, echoing the shape of the mountain. Generous overhangs provide shade and protection from the elements, while allowing the wall below to undulate with bay windows. The house opens to the view through bay windows on the first floor and a band of windows framed by colonnettes in the broad second floor dormer. *Courtesy of © Robert Benson Photography*

The voluminous hipped roof incorporates a second floor but sweeps down to a low eave. A rounded bulge in the eave marks the entry. This curvy variation in an otherwise simple, rectangular hipped roof is an event that gets noticed. *Courtesy of © Robert Benson Photography*

A carved tree trunk, in the rustic spirit of a mountain lodge, supports the entry overhang. The classically inspired, dark green, painted colonnettes of the second floor dormers add an understated sophistication to the rustic house. *Courtesy of © Robert Benson Photography*

The entrance hall is like a broad landing of the stair that spills down two steps into the living room. Stepping down to the living room is a ceremonious gesture that causes the room to seem grander. *Courtesy of © Robert Benson Photography*

The house is entered through a wide, oversized Dutch door with glass in the upper half. The wide, rough-sawn planks on the walls and the flat wooden cutouts for balusters lend a countrified, vernacular feeling to the entrance. *Courtesy of © Robert Benson Photography*

The entrance is uncluttered with closets, but a mudroom opens directly off it through a wide opening. *Courtesy of © Robert Benson Photography*

A mantel shelf on brackets, painted paneling, and colorful tiles frame the fireplace. *Courtesy of © Robert Benson Photography*

The house echoes the sleeping pavilion with local, natural materials, wide overhangs, and a naturally inspired color palette. *Courtesy of © Robert Benson Photography*

Suburban Shingle

This nine-room, Shingle Style house designed and built by Douglas Touart includes element of Arts and Crafts style. Stone columns with tapered cedar posts frame the front windows. The Anderson® 6/1 high performance windows with transoms provide natural sunlight throughout the house. *Courtesy of D. Peter Lund*

The exterior is natural cedar highlighted by the green color palette on the trim and windows. The decorative corbels on the roof are painted to match the trim. *Courtesy of D. Peter Lund*

The hand forged doorknobs, tongue and groove paneling, and built-in bookcases reflect the era of true craftsmanship seen in the beginning days of Shingle Style. *Courtesy of D. Peter Lund*

The living room has wide oak flooring, recessed lighting, and a built-in window seat in the front. Its fireplace is reminiscent of designs by Charles Rennie McIntosh. *Courtesy of D. Peter Lund*

The large open kitchen features extensive storage in Shaker cherry cabinets. The hand built cabinets between the living room and family room include a wet bar and storage. *Courtesy of D. Peter Lund*

The details in this suburban shingle reflect those of the great nineteenth century cottages. *Courtesy of D. Peter Lund*

Twenty-first Century Shingle

David Andreozzi, who views himself as an architect specializing in the traditional variants of Shingle Style, was asked to take that classical order and bring it kicking and screaming into the future. This home's exterior clearly draws its influence from historical New England structures by using time-proven elements like the warm red cedar shingle siding, traditional divided lite windows, and a standing seam copper roof. A heavy stone base that references the local stonewalls grounds it back to earth. The traditional elements are purposely contrasted with a much more contemporary approach to the house's form: a morphed reinterpretation of the Shingle Style archetype in a perfect representation of form follows function. *Courtesy of Aaron Usher III*

The tight, triangular site, coastal restrictions, and myriad local zoning laws dictated the general size and shape of the plan. The clients' desire to accommodate a summer's worth of visitors pushed the house up to three stories. *Courtesy of Aaron Usher III*

It's all about the rooms with views that seem endless. The general layout of the house is a classic "upside-down house" with all the secondary bedrooms on the ground level where it is cooler at night, living areas on the second floor level to capture the day's cooling breezes, and a private master suite and study on the third level for expansive views. Large expanses of glass and exterior porches at all three levels blur the distinction between inside and outside rooms. Overhangs provide a mix of shaded porches and sunny areas. *Courtesy of Aaron Usher III*

The middle level features a radiated great room with a family room, a dining table, and a kitchen, all with equal views of the ocean. *Courtesy of Aaron Usher III*

The open great room and entertaining area looks more like a modern loft than a home design inspired by the New England Shingle Style. *Courtesy of Aaron Usher III*

The radial kitchen design starts with a small desk in the corner and continues along the curve until it abuts the dining room table. The choice of natural woods in the modern flat paneled cabinet doors pays homage to New England's past and present. *Courtesy of Aaron Usher III*

The third-level master suite includes a dramatic vista reminiscent of standing on the bow of the boat. The details are in a simple nautically inspired theme from the arched ceiling to the simple paneled moldings to the understated color palette. *Courtesy of Aaron Usher III*

The entry stair represents the center or the generating radii for the entire house design, as shown in the balcony rail itself. All of this geometry connects the participant to the views at the end of the axis. Also inspired by the ocean, the newel posts reflect the magnificent masts, booms, and decorative woodwork of old ocean vessels. *Courtesy of Aaron Usher III*

The master suite office is flooded with light on three sides and from the cupola centered on the pyramid-shaped cathedral ceiling above. *Courtesy of Aaron Usher III*

Shingle Style Lake Cottages

On a 16-acre site overlooking Wenham Lake in Wenham, MA, this cottage is one of four houses designed by Olson Lewis Dioli & Doktor Architects and built as distinctive interpretations in the Shingle Style.
Photo: Steve Dunwell

In addition to the traditional shingles wrapping around the envelope of each cottage, other architectural details include chimneys, hip roofs, simple dormers, and deep eaves. They lend a diminutive scale to surprisingly large homes. Interiors are bright and light-washed, appointed with modern amenities and spacious living spaces.
Photo: Steve Dunwell

California Craftsman Shingle

Here, Brion Jeanette and Ann Creager have reinterpreted the Shingle Style to allow for greater openness suitable to the California environment and simplified classical craftsmen details. The traditional entry brings the visitor through a gated, private garden to the front door of the house. The open living area enjoys expansive views of the Pacific Ocean. *Courtesy of EricFigge.com*

Designed on one level, this contemporary California shingle enjoys the temperate Southern California climate. The architects extended the interior living space to the porch, doubling the livable square footage for parties or family pleasure. *Courtesy of Jeffrey D. McCoy*

The kitchen is marked by its handcrafted, Shaker cabinets and traditional wood floors, yet embraces the conveniences of modern lifestyle with granite countertops and contemporary lighting and fixtures. *Courtesy of Jeffrey D. McCoy*

Designed with energy conservation in mind, the home maximizes light and ventilation and takes advantage of prevailing breezes to minimize energy usage. This classical home is also designed to provide for today's casual living style. *Courtesy of Jeffrey D. McCoy*

This guesthouse is detached from the main house and discretely tucked behind the entry garden, allowing guests to come and go freely (or not go at all). A bridge links the main house to the carriage house. It also shelters the door to the mudroom. *Courtesy of Jeffrey D. McCoy*

This single-story home wraps completely around the ocean-facing patio, washing the entire house with natural light, ventilation, and unmatched views. *Courtesy of Jeffrey D. McCoy*

Modern Twist

Traditional cedar shingles cover this private, lakeside residence designed by Bergland + Cram. The twist is the modern form of the home, with distinct cubes topped in tidy, fort-like roofs. Windows punch through the exterior, flooding the house with natural light, gorgeous views of the water, and cross ventilation off the lake. An open deck meanders around the spacious lawn leading to the lake, and joins with a covered porch for maximum versatility and use of the outdoor spaces. The main house is 2,448 square feet. When the second house and the bonus space/garage are added, the entire property is over 4,000 square feet. *Courtesy of Joseph Anderson, Bergland + Cram*

Iowa Lakeside

Designed by Bergland + Cram, this lake home maximizes its footprint on a small lot with an axis of circulation flowing from the front door to the lake. A shingled facade grows out of a stone base with the asymmetrical shape of the home camouflaging the garage doors from the street side. *Courtesy of Douglas Foreshoe, Bergland + Cram*

The lakeside takes on a somewhat symmetrical facade, with expansive windows and a variety of outdoor spaces. *Courtesy of Douglas Foreshoe, Bergland + Cram*

Red Oak Mountain

Taking many cues in form, materials, and attitude from the more traditional Shingle Style, Carter+Burton Architecture P.L.C. designed Red Oak Mountain as a modern interpretation of the 100-year-old style. *Courtesy of Daniel Azfal*

The masonry main level, rendered in concrete masonry units (CMU) rather than rough hewn stone, grounds the house to the hillside. The dramatic roof soaring into the treetops is reminiscent of the irregular roof lines of traditional Shingle Style houses. The sleek materials, CMU, horizontal siding, and metal roof, all accentuate the simplicity of the design and the color palette, which is taken from the trees and rocks surrounding the house. *Courtesy of Daniel Azfal*

The proportion of the house is similar to a Shingle Style house: it has the asymmetrical yet boxy shape modeled after rustic cabins and an unornamented surface, which allows the windows to be showcased both inside and out. *Courtesy of Daniel Azfal*

New England Cottage Renovation

Olson Lewis Dioli & Doktor Architects renovated this existing one-story structure into a two-story home. It was built by a general contractor for his own family and truly reflects their love for historic details. The rambling flow of each section of the house depicts one of the key Shingle Style characteristics. *Courtesy of Dan Gair/Blind Dog Photo*

The natural stone and shingles incorporated into the exterior connect the house to its environment. *Courtesy of Dan Gair/Blind Dog Photo*

The plan focuses on a great room, catering to family life, and radiates out to include both casual living and formal public rooms. Articulation of porches in the front and back defines the connection between the indoor and outdoor spaces. *Courtesy of Dan Gair/Blind Dog Photo*

The Unbuildable Lot

Perched high on the rocky coast in Ogunquit, Maine, is a Shingle Style cottage designed in 2007 by Ralf Amsden of Living Spaces Architectural Associates. This 2,900-square-foot gem was built on a piece of land considered unbuildable. The setbacks from the ocean and property lines created a narrow, angular squiggle of a footprint only twenty feet wide in places. *Courtesy of Veodao Nu Bunnag*

A mix of Maine seacoast styling with a hint of Victorian features blends this house into the shoreline. The unsurpassed view warranted a supreme effort to create a home large enough to live in and take full advantage of the location. *Courtesy of Veodao Nu Bunnag*

As it worked out, a plan evolved that manifested an open kitchen, dining, and living area on the first floor. The long site lines create an illusion of size. *Courtesy of Veodao Nu Bunnag*

A formal dining room is tucked in on one end and a beautiful mahogany-paneled den on the other. An arched entrance supported by columns on pedestal bases frames the den. *Courtesy of Veodao Nu Bunnag*

The second floor offers a gracious master bedroom suite with a sitting area and an outdoor roof deck beyond the French doors. The octagonal master bedroom has a wood-paneled, cathedral ceiling. *Courtesy of Veodao Nu Bunnag*

The master bedroom fireplace has a raised hearth and diamond grilled windows above to compliment the window seat. *Courtesy of Veodao Nu Bunnag*

The winding footprint sets the house up to experience the full beauty of the view, which includes rocky coasts in both directions. In addition, one could watch the boats pass by as they entered the harbor. Because of the restrictions, no true patio or deck could be on the first floor level, but a lush lawn with landscaping was a good alternative. *Courtesy of Veodao Nu Bunnag*

Shingles of Merit

We often think of shingle houses as being grandiose in size. Untrue. There are many charming smaller ones that we can appreciate for their simplicity, symmetry, and integrity. They represent an old-fashioned simplicity in this dot com world, where even the microwave takes too long.

Guest House/ Garage

This Shingle Style lakeside home consists of guest quarters over a four-bay garage and workshop. J.S. MacPhee Company Architects designed it to create a space on the client's property for use during and after reconstruction of the existing summer cottage. The surrounding property was left mostly untouched, but additional swales and contours were created to minimize run-off and reduce the potential for erosion into the lake. *Courtesy of J. S. McPhee Company/Architects*

Bunkrooms provide additional space for extended family and friends. A large dining area and living room provide ample space for everyone to gather and enjoy views of the lake and mountains beyond. *Courtesy of J. S. McPhee Company/Architects*

The building was designed as a low-cost, energy-efficient, year-round vacation home. The walls and roof are insulated with open-cell foam. A tankless water heater provides hot water, and a high-efficiency, wall-hung boiler supports baseboard heating. Low-E glass, deep roof overhangs, and the building's orientation help protect the living space from solar gain. *Courtesy of J. S. McPhee Company/Architects*

Highland Cottage

Nestled up alongside an accompanying pool, this charming cottage, designed by Gleysteen Design LLC, contains two bedrooms, a small kitchen, and a great room terminated by a towering stone fireplace and chimney. *Photo by Marcus Gleysteen*

The towering stone chimney, with articulated stonework, pushes through a grid of windows and floats above a lower garage, which resembles a large outdoor fireplace. *Photo by Marcus Gleysteen*

A rotunda-like porch transitions to a pergola along the front of the cottage. *Photo by Marcus Gleysteen*

The glass folding-walls of the cottage accordion open to make the outdoors feel like an extension of the living space. *Photo by Marcus Gleysteen*

The round form is found again on the back of the cottage protruding as the stair tower. This street-facing elevation has a high stone base for privacy, detailed with buttresses. *Photo by Marcus Gleysteen*

Inside, the great room contains a large beautiful timber frame, an even larger stone fireplace and chimney, and a folding glass wall that opens out to the pool. *Photo by Marcus Gleysteen*

The airy fir ceiling adds warmth to the cozy cottage. *Photo by Marcus Gleysteen*

Shingle in the Woods

Craig Capone of Russell Scott Steedle & Capone Architects designed for himself a small house on the southern coast of Maine. Built in 2007, the cedar shake clad exterior borrows from the local Shingle Style tradition of varied massing, incorporating various gables, bays, grouped windows, and porches. *Courtesy of Craig Capone*

The house is situated in the woods. The trees give it shade from the sun in the summer while allowing the winter sun to warm the rooms inside through the many south-facing windows. The stone retaining walls, porches, and decks help tie the house to the ground and allow the living space to extend outside in the warm summer months. *Courtesy of Craig Capone*

The approach to the house passes through a garden and onto a deck in dappled sunlight, which reinforces the house's relationship to nature. *Courtesy of Craig Capone*

Inside the house is a less traditional layout of rooms. The living spaces flow into one another in a loose east/west access that allows every room to have southern sunlight. A reference to the Shingle Style tradition has the main staircase opposite the front door, spilling down into the front entryway of the house. *Courtesy of Craig Capone*

Light tones were used on the walls, and wood was used throughout the house to give it a warm and bright feel. Here a cozy den overlooks the living room below. *Courtesy of Craig Capone*

The rooms have an overlay of Arts and Crafts detailing. A wood stove provides supplemental heat in winter and provides a focal point in the living room. *Courtesy of Craig Capone*

Another tradition borrowed from coastal summerhouses is the sleeping porch. This one is directly off the second floor master bedroom. Its three screened walls, with the woods immediately beyond, give it the feeling of a tree house. *Courtesy of Craig Capone*

Maine "Down East" Shingle Style Cabins

Olson Lewis Dioli & Doktor Architects captured the classic "Maine Lodge" architecture in this 16-home, year-round community setting. Each 1,800-square-foot camp provides private and public opportunities and was designed to blend with its surrounding natural landscapes. *Courtesy of Todd Caverly*

Exterior details include cedar shingles and color coordinating trim, creating a consistent look and feel throughout the community. *Courtesy of Todd Caverly*

Shingle Style characteristics include the open interior floor plan, which maximizes the living spaces and offers details that create a warm environment for the homeowners.
Courtesy of Todd Caverly

Mattapoisett Shingle

J. S. McPhee Company/Architects designed this house for a couple who decided to leave their suburban Boston neighborhood and move to the shore. Here, they enjoy the ocean year-round and their sailboat is moored close by. The existing cottage, which formed the front portion of the house, was completely renovated. Numerous ad hoc additions were removed from the back of the house, and a new two-story volume was added. A new kitchen, eating space, and mudroom on the first floor are connected by a stair tower, which leads to the second floor master suite and a viewing area above the roof. The tower provides glimpses of the ocean over the peaks of the surrounding homes. *Courtesy of J. S. McPhee Company/Architects*

Lake Library

This is a folly, a miniature castle. Albert, Righter & Tittman squeezed elements derived from the Shingle Style together vertically, erupting in a fantastical roofscape of light monitor, chimney, and turret. A new 900-square- foot out-building, it accompanies a 100-year-old lakeside vacation house. *Courtesy of Greg Premru*

This complete one-bedroom house serves as a retreat and library for either the owners or their guests and provides an ideal vantage point for watching games on the adjacent tennis court. The main level includes a deck that overlooks the old clay tennis court, a double-height living room, and a bathroom. A flap of cedar shingles sweeps out from the wall to shelter the entry. The 100-year-old main house sprawls across the lakefront, but Lake Library stands up vertically against a backdrop of tall pines. *Courtesy of Greg Premru*

A grand, two-story high oriel window fills the south side and faces a view of the lake. The cedar shingle walls and roof, the dark green exterior rim, and the natural wood interior are consistent with the main house, but Lake Library has its own exuberant flavor. *Courtesy of Greg Premru*

Brackets support the oriel window above, which does not meet the ground because zoning restrictions limited the size of the building's footprint. *Courtesy of Greg Premru*

The lodge-like living room accounts for more than half the volume of the interior. The massive fireplace of local granite is a focal point of the room. *Courtesy of Greg Premru*

The height of the space and the upward sweep of the vertical oriel window impart grandeur, but the warmth of the unfinished pine paneling and the rusticity of the trim details, which are cut in the angular manner of Adirondack camps, temper it. *Courtesy of Greg Premru*

The living room is flooded with light from the south-facing oriel window and from the light monitor above. The motorized awning windows in the light monitor open for natural ventilation and are supplemented by a fan. *Courtesy of Greg Premru*

The circular stair connects the three floors, snaking around the inside of its round tower without a supporting center post. Running your hand along the sinuous, continuous wooden rail is a pleasant tactile experience. *Courtesy of Greg Premru*

The cozy second-floor bedroom is tucked under the eave, with a band of small windows wrapping around two sides. As this room is the only space on the second floor, the client felt that a door was unnecessary. Instead, a screen of turned colonnettes separates the stairs from the bedroom. *Courtesy of Greg Premru*

A Small Shingle House

After years of living in an apartment in the city, collecting Arts and Crafts artwork and furnishings, and dreaming of a home for themselves and their belongings, the client contacted André G. Fontaine Architect about designing such a home. The couple had already purchased a 12-acre wooded parcel of land with views down to a river that traversed the south and east boundaries. Because the property was adjacent to a state park, it also had a large environmental buffer. This buffer precluded siting the house as close to the water as the client would have liked, but after walking the property, a quite reasonable location with good views and solar orientation was selected. Because the client indicated that they would spend the most time in the kitchen and breakfast area, those spaces were provided with the best views and orientation on the southeast corner of the house, as shown here. *Courtesy of Anne Gummerson Photography*

This view of the west side of the house shows the extended entry porch and inglenook fireplace chimney beyond. The inglenook, with its Rumford fireplace, is located to the north. The balance of the 1,100-square-foot first floor is composed of a combined living and dining room, a foyer, powder room, and miscellaneous service areas. *Courtesy of Anne Gummerson Photography*

Their program also called for a porch open to a grassy area for supervising children at play, as well as a screened porch for entertaining and enjoying a bug-free outdoors. *Courtesy of Anne Gummerson Photography*

The breakfast room has a trellis and window boxes. *Courtesy of Anne Gummerson Photography*

The foyer includes the powder room and the stairs to the second floor. *Courtesy of Anne Gummerson Photography*

The combined living-dining room is open to the kitchen and breakfast room. *Courtesy of Anne Gummerson Photography*

Windows flood light into the second floor hallway. The 1,125-square-foot second floor encompasses a master suite, second bedroom/office, and a suite for two children. The children's area is unique in that each child has a rather small bed alcove with built-ins for their personal items along with a common play area, where the computer and television are located. *Courtesy of Anne Gummerson Photography*

In this view into the combined living-dining room from the kitchen, the door on the left leads out to the west entry porch. The openings beyond lead to the fireplace inglenook. Note the stained, exposed second floor structure at the ceiling. *Courtesy of Anne Gummerson Photography*

The inglenook contains an energy-saving Rumford fireplace with a tile surround and hearth. *Courtesy of Anne Gummerson Photography*

Shingle Family House

This gut-renovation by I-Kanda Architects (in collaboration with owner/builder Flatcut) converted a derelict single-family house into a "shingle family" house, promoting a sustainable approach to design and construction. *Courtesy of I-Kanda Architects*

A tall, narrow opening on the side provides access and creates a framed view of the side yard. *Courtesy of I-Kanda Architects*

The concrete slab for the ground level was poured-in-place directly inside the existing foundation walls, eliminating the need for formwork. In fact, much of the perimeter wall of the first floor was kept intact and simply re-clad with new shingles. The new second floor and roof sit on top of the original concrete block structure. Two simple CMU walls partially enclose the rest of the site, creating a sense of privacy within the expansive yard. *Courtesy of I-Kanda Architects*

The oversized overhang on the west facade shades against low afternoon sun and simultaneously creates a breezeway along the side of the house. A large opening on top aligns with a picture window on the second floor, acting like a skylight to pull natural light down into the central stairwell. *Courtesy of I-Kanda Architects*

On the interior, a central core contains all the essentials for a two-bedroom house: stairs, kitchen, 2-1/2 bathrooms, and a stacked washer/dryer. All the associated mechanicals are also located here, including an energy saving tankless water heater. The small square footage of the house allows efficient usage of the central heat/AC system, requiring almost no ductwork. All materials and trades were locally sourced within a 50-mile radius, including windows, lumber, and shingles. *Courtesy of I-Kanda Architects*

Biddeford Vacation Home

J. S. McPhee Company/Architects designed this Maine coast home to fit the existing footprint of a modest fisherman's cottage yet provide generous space through its open floor plan and expansive second floor. Where a two-car garage was once connected through a modest breezeway, there is now an open, airy family room with a master bedroom suite above. A wrap-around porch along the front of the house provides a wonderful place to sit and enjoy the coast. It includes a screened room where family and friends often gather for meals. *Courtesy of J. S. McPhee Company/Architects*

A rear entry porch creates a pleasant spot to brush off sand from the beach, as well as a peaceful setting to sit and visit or just read a book. *Courtesy of J. S. McPhee Company/Architects*

Classic Shingle Style details help define the pleasant character of this home and tie it to the fabric of the surrounding neighborhood. The steeply pitched gables, large shed dormers, bleached cedar shingles, and whitewash painted trim are all traditional elements of Maine's coast. *Courtesy of J. S. McPhee Company/Architects*

Institutional & Commercial Shingles

Recently, architects and builders have begun using Shingle Style in institutional and commercial buildings.

The East 6th Street House

The East 6th Street House is a speculative residential unit, designed by Touloukian Touloukian Inc., at the rear of an urban lot. There the building code prevents windows on two of the four facades, and restricted views limit visibility to the street and to desirable adjacent properties. The site is a long narrow parcel with minimal street frontage. The design includes the renovation of the brick bow front (circa 1890) into two residential units at the front of the lot, the demolition of a "post war" wood frame addition at the rear of the lot, and the construction of a one-unit residential addition over most of the remaining existing foundation. *Photo by Stephen Lee Architectural Photography*

On the exterior, the neighborhood context of boxlike structures with varied siding patterns is re-interpreted through simple geometric volumes and the siding pattern of fiber-cement clapboard in various standard widths. *Photo by Stephen Lee Architectural Photography*

A dramatic response to the site, the design includes a three-story skylight shaft at the "dark" corner of the addition (where no windows are allowed) to bring light to every floor and into the kitchen, study, and master bathroom. A dramatic "skylight hall" with minimal windows on the exterior wall redirects the focus away from views to the adjacent rear lot and towards a modern, sun-filled spacious environment. *Photo by Stephen Lee Architectural Photography*

The top floor skylight hall has painted plaster light shafts, translucent glass and steel handrail system, and birch casework. *Photo by Stephen Lee Architectural Photography*

Top floor skylight hall has a freestanding column and operable corner windows. *Photo by Stephen Lee Architectural Photography*

First floor light shaft at kitchen has granite counters and back splash and stainless steel shelves. *Photo by Stephen Lee Architectural Photography*

Congregation B'nai Shalom

William Sloan Associates designed a new Shingle Style sanctuary and Hebrew School for a growing congregation in Westborough, Massachusetts. This 16,000-square-foot addition is organized around a new courtyard with new lobby, office, and classroom space, as well as a new 400-seat sanctuary. *Courtesy of William Sloan*

Key to the design is a sunny sanctuary set at a slight angle to the street, facing the congregation eastward towards Jerusalem, with the entrance oriented towards the community of Westborough. Linking the sanctuary to the original building, a new classroom wing forms a courtyard that unites all elements of the synagogue. The character of the structure, both inside and out, reflects a "walk in the woods," with simple wood cladding, a warm, earthy color palette, and the pine boards of the sanctuary lending warmth to the sounds of voices and music. *Courtesy of William Sloan*

Evoking memories of the synagogues of Eastern Europe, the sanctuary and Hebrew School are a combination of red cedar shingle and stucco. Typically, the stucco extends from grade to the first floor ceiling level, with shingles above, including dormers and gable ends. At the sanctuary, the shingle extends to the first floor window stools, set just above eye level. *Courtesy of William Sloan*

Simple Shingle Style Sets Sail

Although integrally tied to its resort community, this long-time sailing group had never had a home base for meetings, conducting classes for beginners in the sport, or for equipment storage. Bergland + Cram designed a new Shingle Style facility for the group.

After negotiating with the community, the group obtained a piece of property in a highly visible location, prized for its access to downtown and the lake. The owners required a simple, low maintenance facility that would be suitable and would effectively eliminate a major drive through the lakefront area. *Courtesy of Douglas Foreshoe, Bergland + Cram*

The new facility is also intended to draw attention to the group's activities, thereby encouraging interest in the community for the sport of sailing. *Courtesy of Douglas Foreshoe, Bergland + Cram*

Temple Shir Tikvah

As the first synagogue in Winchester, the congregation's goal was to achieve a flexible worship and educational building and to create a new image for the temple in the community. An adaptive reuse project, William Sloan Associates used a former apartment building to create a new Shingle Style image, which expressed this new use in a traditional statement familiar to the congregation and the community. Its overall architectural character incorporates traditional elements evocative of the wooden synagogues of Poland and the schuls of Eastern Europe within an American architectural vocabulary. *Courtesy of William Sloan*

The design of the approximately 7,500-square-foot, three-story structure illustrates a number of traditions in its architecture. This wood frame building respects the architecture of its residential neighbors, predominantly single-family houses, by its use of wood shingle siding and wood windows, with the appropriate detailing of water tables and eaves. At the same time, the design asserts itself as an important institution of public assembly in the Town of Winchester by employing more monumental traditions, such as a large, sheltering slate roof and broad entrance portals. Here, diamond shingles were used as infill within a pair of diamond light windows. *Courtesy of William Sloan*

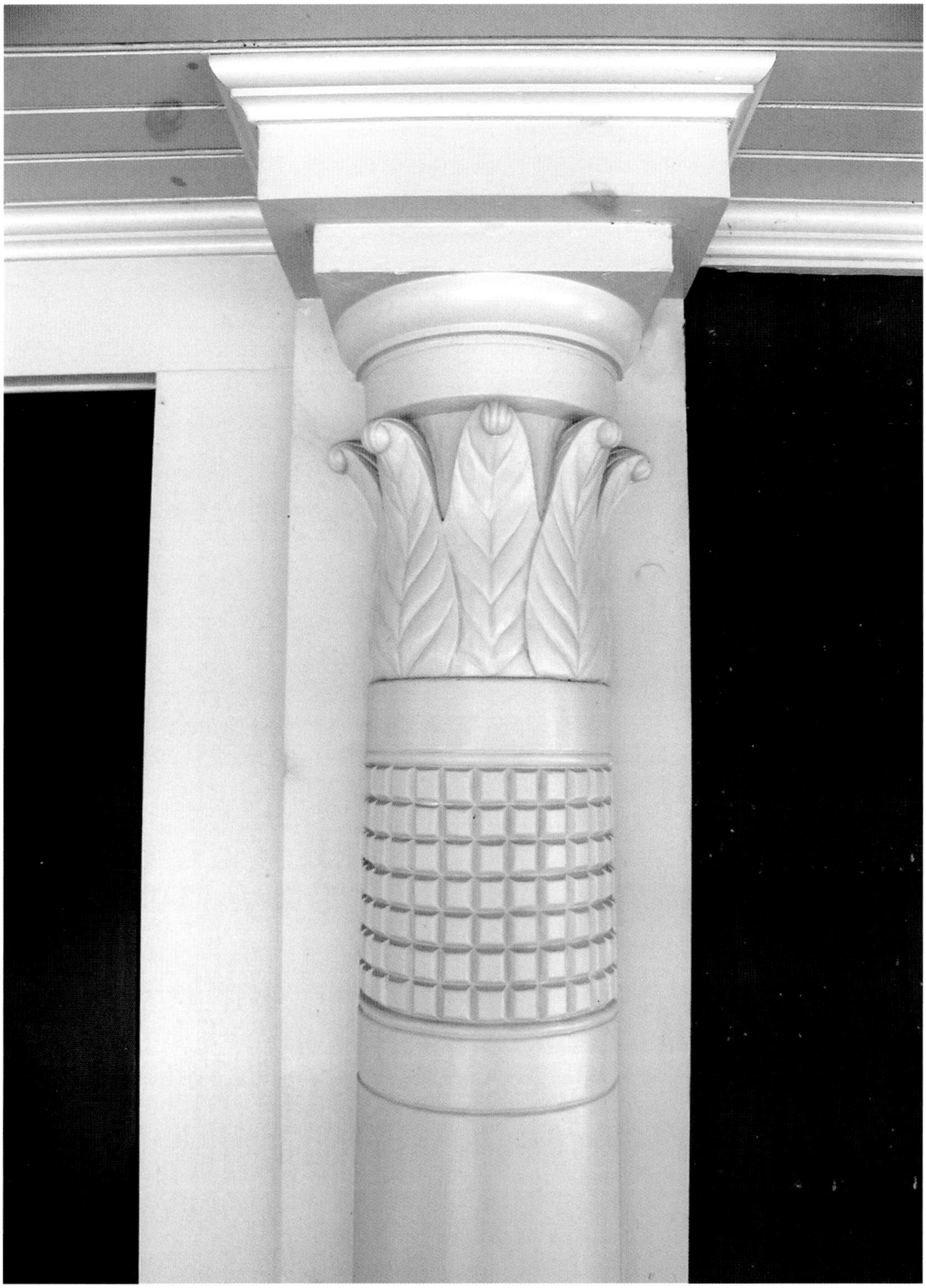

But the most important tradition that this religious building must respect is that of a Reform Jewish congregation, of gathering, of education, of prayer, and of worship. The simple upper row of round top windows reflects the upper level sanctuary. The simple strong form of the slate roof and broad overhang protects the gathering space beneath. The welcoming porches and balconies are supported by familiar columns, some modeled after those of the Temple of Solomon, the first house of worship described in the scriptures. *Courtesy of William Sloan*

Nehoiden House at Wellesley College

William Sloan Associates designed the Nehoiden House as a residence for the administrative vice-president of Wellesley College. Currently, it provides approximately 5,000 square feet of office space for the college's Department of Resources. The stucco and shingle design of the structure complements the historic French House across the fairway. *Photograph: ©2009 Warren Patterson Photography*

Exterior materials are stucco; red cedar shingles; and redwood rafters, rafter tails, and bargeboards. The primary siding material is stained shingles, with three stucco gables that step back along the first fairway of Nehoiden Golf Club. *Courtesy of William Sloan*

Resources

Founded in 1971, **Albert, Righter & Tittmann Architects** offers complete architectural services for projects of many types and sizes, including museums, libraries, and many houses big and small throughout New England and New York. The partnership was founded on shared backgrounds and interests. All members of the firm contribute their knowledge of design, sustainability issues, project management, and construction administration to the design process. They emphasize the appropriateness of a design to its setting and the craft of making buildings. They believe that design can incorporate the continuity of traditions and the excitement of the new. They experiment with stylistic rules as a means to cherish the past without being limited by it.

8 Winter Street, 3rd Floor
Boston, MA 02108
1-617-451-5740
email@alriti.com
www.alriti.com

For over 25 years, the residential architectural firm of **André G. Fontaine Architects** has been committed to the guiding principle of dwelling and environmental unity by creating contextual architecture, winning numerous awards in the process. Published widely over the years in the architectural press and on HGTV, the firm looks forward to continuing its pursuit of finely honed solutions for its clients; for example, a green roof multi-level screened porch for a life-long gardening devotee. The firm's studio, located in the Maryland countryside, continues to provide a contemplative setting in which to focus on innovative design concepts and environmentally sound solutions worked out in close collaboration with its clients.

PO Box 357
Glenelg, MD 21737
1-410-531-3925
ogeearch@aol.com

Andreozzi Architects, a team of design-oriented architects, concentrates in high-end, custom residential architecture. The diversity of the firm's work ranges from historic reproduction and reinterpretation to state-of-the-art modern architecture. It offers individually designed moldings, millwork, and masonry while focusing on creating architecture that integrates into the landscape design as strongly as the interior design. Its work includes award-winning Shingle Style residences designed and built along New England's shoreline, as well as custom residences from Providence's East Side to the shorelines throughout Rhode Island and Massachusetts.

232D Waseca Avenue
Barrington, RI 02806
1-401-245-6800
dsra@andreozzi.com
www.andreozzi.com

Bergland + Cram (B + C) is a leading north Iowa multi-service architectural firm. Its team of twelve professionals provides creative, functional design throughout the Midwest. Its interest in a variety of projects stems from its long-standing commitment to community development fueled by its dedication to creative, functional design. The firm has built its practice on the importance of client relationships and takes pride in the way in which it celebrates every step of the design process. Its service is backed by past experience and industry knowledge as well as organization and planning skills.

10002 East State Street
Mason, City, IA 50401
1-641-423-6349
info@berglandandcram.com
www.berglandandcram.com

Brion Jeannette Architecture began in 1974 with a design philosophy focused on green architecture. The firm has spent 30+ years incorporating healthy building products, implementing passive and active solar strategies, and employing these techniques, generally without visible notice. Its projects range in scope from 2,500 square foot beach cottages to palaces around the world.

470 Old Newport Boulevard
Newport Beach, CA 92663
1-949-645-5854
www.customarchitecture.com

Carter+Burton Architecture P.L.C. is a small Virginia architecture firm that specializes in a few good projects per year. Located in Berryville, a small town one hour west of Washington, DC, its architects enjoy designing and working within a wide range of budgets. The firm's focus is on quality, craftsmanship, and innovation. It tries to promote passive solar techniques and eco-friendly building materials.

11 W. Main Street
Berryville, VA 22611
1-540-955-1644
jim@carterburton.com
www.carterburton.com

With over 35 years' experience, **Douglas Touart Design and Construction** has been building for those who invest not just in a home, but a way of living. Classic architectural styles, generous floor plans, sound construction, and quality materials are the hallmarks of his hands-on approach to home design and construction principles. Touart not only personally designs and builds each dwelling along with his highly skilled crew, he understands the attention to detail and workmanship that is required to not only make a house a home but also part of a community.

71 Page Road
Bedford, MA 01730
1-781-275-7941

Founded in 1987, **Fellner Associates Architects (FAA)** is committed to the development of responsive architectural solutions. George Fellner, AIA, LEED AP, believes that design is a multi-faceted, evolutionary process. In order to produce responsive architectural solutions, the juxtaposition of context, semantics, sustainability, and pragmatics is sensitively balanced. This integrated choreography reveals that a building has the inherent potential to transcend beyond its physical realm. Thus, there is an opportunity for architecture to not only form a solution, but also to significantly communicate at many levels. As cochairman of the AIA Connecticut Committee on the Environment, Fellner is responsible for developing programs and workshops related to sustainability, including alternative technologies and materials. He has written and lectured extensively on sustainable design strategies, including geothermal systems, environmental subjects, and architectural design.

415 Killingworth Road
Higganum, CT 06441
1-860-345-7558
fellnerarchitects@sbcglobal.net
www.fellnerarchitects.com

Led by architect Marcus Gleysteen, the residential architectural firm **Gleysteen Design** combines artistic vision with the highest professional skill and discipline. The vast majority of their houses in the Boston area, either new construction or renovation, are designed for everyday family use. Each design is honed to be as highly efficient, cost effective, practical, and sustainable as possible. The firm works throughout New England and has recently completed projects as far afield as Carmel, California. Its work reflects an understanding of New England's cultural heritage while integrating current stylistic, functional, and pragmatic needs. The portfolio of the firm showcases a stylistic range that underscores its deep understanding of the principles of home design: performance, livability, and comfort.

185 Mt. Auburn Street
Cambridge, MA 02138
1-617-492-6060
info@gleysteendesign.com
www.gleysteendesign.com

Isamu Kanda of **I-Kanda Architects** earned an M. Arch from Harvard Graduate School of Design and a B.S. in Structural Engineering from Cornell University. His experience ranges from structural engineering, architecture, and construction, to timber frame carpentry. He has worked on projects ranging in scale from infrastructural, institutional, and commercial to residential and furniture, but he always applies his background to promote full involvement and collaboration between disciplines to create thoughtful, responsible design solutions.

364 Main Street
Charlestown, MA 02129
1-646-228-1040
info@i-kanda.com
www.i-kanda.com

J.S. MacPhee Company | Architects has built a reputation for providing uncompromising quality, creativity, and a high level of client-focused service. Specializing in residential, commercial, and academic architecture, the firm's expertise ranges from regional vernacular to innovative contemporary design.

77 Commonwealth Avenue
Concord, MA 01742
1-978-287-0113
www.jsmacphee.com

Living Spaces Architectural Associates began as a design-build firm dedicated to energy efficient solar design. After designing several active solar homes, it moved into the passive solar design period. During the 1980s, Crown Publications of New York accepted six of its designs for passive solar homes. Currently, the firm places more emphasis on affordable methods of building, energy conservation, maintenance free specifications, and realistic sizing of home plans.

1247 Washington Road
Rye, NH 03870
1-603-964-5180
livingspacesllc@comcast.net
www.livingspacesarchitects.com

Mark Chaney Architects is an interdisciplinary firm integrating digital media and full service architectural design with experience in residential, educational, luxury resort, commercial office, interior design, and master planning projects of every size. It strives to achieve a balance between inspiring sustainable design, accurate timely schedules, and affordable regional materials and techniques. Its project teams are coordinated to instill a mutual respect and trust between like-minded clients and consultants. The firm has fun with the process of design yet understands its future depends on exceeding the quality controls and standards of excellence it infuses into every project.

4050 Williston Road
South Burlington, VT 05403
1-802-733-7657
www.mcarch.net

Mitchell Wilk Architecture PC is an innovative, full-service architectural firm based on the belief that architecture should strive to enrich the lives of those who come into contact with it. Founded by Douglas Wilk, the firm has earned a reputation for developing innovative, carefully considered, and well-detailed designs. It believes that successful design is based upon an inherent respect for proportion, material, light, and composition that integrates itself seamlessly with function to meet the clients' varying needs and aesthetic desires. The homes produced by the firm vary in style and expression to reflect its clients' unique set of expectations, site context, budget, and schedule.

31 Purchase Street
Rye, NY 10580
1-914-925-0107

Nantucket Architecture Group designs buildings, spaces, and environments for residential and commercial clients on the Cape and the Islands. It has developed a reputation for spaces and buildings that respect and enhance a client's lifestyle and dreams; its integration of outdoor and indoor spaces in an environmentally sensitive manner; and its focus on simple lines, classical forms, historic details, unusual materials, fun, intimacy, comfort, and spaciousness. Many of its projects incorporate green architectural methods, materials, and systems that help reduce impacts on the environment.

P.O. Box 1814
Nantucket, MA 02554
1-508-228-5631
nag@nantucket.net
www.nantucketarchitecture.com

Located in centuries-old Manchester-by-the-Sea, **Olson Lewis Dioli & Doktor Architects (OLD&D)** is a full- service, multi-discipline architectural firm whose design process is a collaborative one. They work in partnership with their clients, listening closely, to develop architectural solutions that fully support every client's goals and aspirations. Their award-winning work raises a client's expectations off the page and builds it into every detail. OLD&D's areas of expertise include residential, hospitality, education, and life sciences. They believe in architecture that functions well, is appropriate to its intent, pleases the people who use and live in its spaces, and reflects clarity of design and the highest of artistic concepts. The firm is especially known for its regional design.

17 Elm Street
Manchester-by-the-Sea, MA 01944
1-978-526-4386
architect@oldarch.com
www.oldarch.com

R. S. Granoff Architects is a full-service architecture, planning, and interior design firm dedicated to providing outstanding client service and achieving excellence in architecture. With offices in Greenwich, Connecticut, and Southampton, New York, the firm works on a wide variety of residential and commercial projects throughout the New York metropolitan area. It incorporates human-centered, sustainable design principles into all of its projects and has extensive experience with solar energy, geothermal systems, and high-efficiency lighting. Its philosophy of architecture is balanced between respect for the past and excitement about the future, which has resulted in work of great variety, vitality, and enduring quality.

30 West Putnam Avenue
Greenwich, CT 06830
1-203-625-9460
rg@granoffarchitects.com
www.granoffarchitects.com

Robert Storm Architects (RSA), founded twenty years ago, has focused on excellence in the design and management of residential architecture projects. Its work has appeared in Home Magazine, Westport Magazine, and House Beautiful, Kitchen and Bath. The majority of RSA's projects are in Westport, Connecticut, and East Hampton, New York. The firm's approach begins with the client's aspirations, enabling them to benefit from its professional experience while feeling included in the process. Many projects are derived from vernacular or historical vocabularies that best suit a project's context. The European Arts and Crafts and American Shingle Style particularly influence the firm's work.

315 Main Street
Westport, CT 06880
1-203-222-9055
www.ArchitectStorm.com

Russell Scott Steedle & Capone Architects Inc. is a small architectural firm in Cambridge, Massachusetts, specializing in the design of multi-family housing, including both new construction and historic renovation. Other work has included private homes and medical and commercial projects throughout New England. The firm also has unique expertise in the design of book storage facilities for such clients as Harvard, Yale, Princeton, Columbia, Brown, and Cornell Universities.

18 Brattle Street
Cambridge, MA 02138
1-617-661-5880
www.rssc-architects.com

Touloukian Touloukian Inc. is an award-winning architectural and urban design firm located in downtown Boston. It offers a broad range of architectural, interior design, and urban planning services. Through ongoing collaboration with its clients, the firm achieves a contextually relevant and sensitive architecture solution that works. Perceiving the design process as a creative catalyst for new opportunities, its goal is to provide intelligent, diverse, and incisive solutions to design problems. Through working with many other professionals, its result can be a project that is a harmonious balance of all parts of art, function, and utility.

153 Milk Street, Suite 202
Boston, MA 02109
1-617-526-0884
ttouloukian@cs.com
www.ttarch.com

Founded in 1987, **William Sloan Associates (WSA)** designs projects for education, worship, the arts, residences, and historic renovations. In all projects, it strives to accomplish solid and simple yet powerful design solutions that will stand the test of time. It believes the most sustainable design is the design that sustains. Throughout eastern Massachusetts, this work has often been executed in a wood frame vocabulary with wood shingles as a key exterior material. WSA is currently the architect for renovations to Stonehurst, The Robert Treat Paine Estate, a landmark Shingle Style residence designed by Henry Hobson Richardson. In March of 2009, WSA won the Traditional Building Design Challenge Award at the Hynes Convention Center. The design task was to design a new residential block that would integrate flawlessly with the historic architecture of Salem, Massachusetts.

551 Main Street
Winchester, MA 01890
1-781-729-2910
chip@williamsloan.com
www.williamsloan.com

Index